D1243934

Monumental
PRAYERS

14 DAYS OF PRAYER INSPIRED BY THE FAITH OF THE PILGRIMS

Michelle Gallagher

"Your prayers... have come up as a memorial
offering before God." - Acts 10:4

Copyright ©2023 - All Rights Reserved

Monumental Prayers is published by Proclamation House, Inc.

Printed in the United States of America

ISBN 978-1-7379016-3-1

Monumental Prayers is adapted from material contained in the
Forefathers Monument Guidebook. No part of either publication
may be reproduced in any form without written permission from the
publisher, except in the case of brief quotations in articles and
reviews with proper attribution.

Layout and design by Michelle Gallagher

PROCLAMATION HOUSE, INC.

A 501(c)(3) non-profit organization.

For information about bulk orders, contact:

Proclamation House, Inc.
6 Main Street Ext #3554, Plymouth, MA 02361
Tel: (774) 766-7122   Email: info@proclamationhouse.org
www.ProclamationHouse.org

Dedication

To my mother, Judith.
Thank you for your powerful
example of prayer in my life, and
your enduring legacy of faith.
I love you.

Foreword

The millions of Christians committed to praying God's will for America today are the harvest of the seeds sown by the Pilgrims, who courageously risked all on a new land and a new kind of government. Their heritage of faith, of religious freedom, and of biblical governance flowed into the Founders as they drafted the Declaration of Independence and the Constitution.

This indelible imprint on our nation fuels the prayers of people today. As President/CEO of Intercessors for America (IFA), I see the legacy of the Pilgrims daily in the prayers of our community, as we pray for biblical values in our laws and government. In fact, IFA was founded 50 years ago in response to *Shaping History Through Prayer and Fasting*, by Derek Prince, which addressed the Pilgrim legacy. He and a group of like-minded men formed IFA to pray fervently for the nation after the disastrous Roe v. Wade decision and in the midst of the Watergate crisis, the sexual revolution, and the Vietnam War. So indebted to the Pilgrims were these men that they based and incorporated IFA in Plymouth, Massachusetts.

A few years ago, one of our staff, Tom Sampley, called one of our intercessors, Michelle Gallagher, to ask how he could pray for her. They prayed together and after their call, Michelle sent Tom this devotional along with a copy of her book, the *Forefathers Monument Guidebook* (ordering information can be found at the back of this book). Tom then showed them to me, and I immediately connected with the beautiful graphics and insightful content. We approached Michelle to create a special edition of *Monumental Prayers* for IFA's 50th anniversary in 2023, and this book is the result.

I had visited Plymouth some years before and was taken aback by the ways the tour guide had falsely, and perhaps unwittingly, removed faith from the story of the Pilgrims. Michelle's books are exactly what we need at a time when the culture at large is questioning and misrepresenting our heritage. The National Monument to the Forefathers in Plymouth is probably the most important monument you may never have heard about. It celebrates the biblical foundations that intercessors are longing for this nation to uphold once again. This devotional takes us on a spiritual tour of this beautiful and profound work of art and civic leadership that reflects the biblical ideals that birthed this nation. It also corrects the historical inaccuracies that have become popular in our day.

When I met Michelle, I knew that IFA had to partner with her to share this devotional with our community. I have often said that IFA is a community of experts – a community whose strength is in the hundreds of thousands of intercessors, much more so than in the staff of roughly 100. Michelle is a perfect example of this. As a resident of Plymouth and one who is praying for her community, she had a vision of what she could do to celebrate the Pilgrim legacy and help equip the rest of us to pray into the rich inheritance we have all received through them. Michelle is one of the foremost experts on the Forefathers Monument, and we receive the blessing.

Faith. Morality. Law. Education. Liberty. These are the cornerstones of the free society the Pilgrims established at Plymouth Colony, and they remain just as vital for us to understand, and pray about, today.

Dave Kubal
President/CEO, Intercessors for America

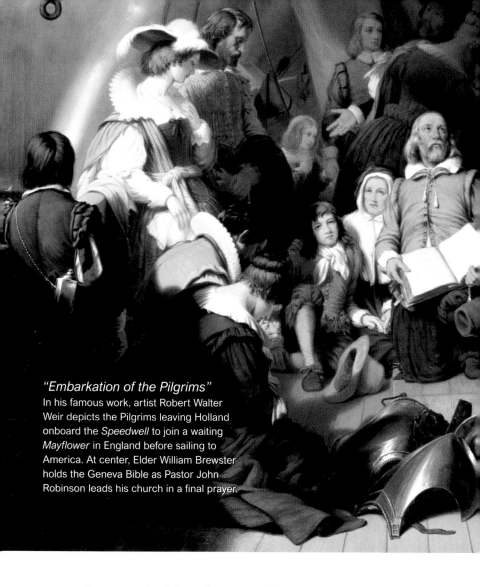

"Embarkation of the Pilgrims"

In his famous work, artist Robert Walter Weir depicts the Pilgrims leaving Holland onboard the *Speedwell* to join a waiting *Mayflower* in England before sailing to America. At center, Elder William Brewster holds the Geneva Bible as Pastor John Robinson leads his church in a final prayer.

"It was replied that all great and honorable actions are accompanied with great difficulties, and must be both met and overcome with answerable courage. It was granted the dangers were great, but not desperate; the difficulties were many, but not invincible. For many of the things feared might never befall; others, by provident care and the use of good means, might in a great measure be prevented; and all of them, through the help of God, by fortitude and patience, might either be borne or overcome.

True it was that such attempts were not to be undertaken without good ground and reason, rashly or lightly; or, as many had done, for curiosity or hope of gain. But their condition was not ordinary; their ends were good and honorable; their calling, lawful and urgent; therefore they might expect the blessing of God on their proceedings. Yea, though they should lose their lives in this action, yet might they have the comfort in knowing that their endeavor was worthy." ~ William Bradford

Introduction

In the introduction to *Forefathers Monument Guidebook,* I share the story of how I first encountered this intriguing monument several years ago. I was fascinated by it, and in time became convinced that God wanted me to use this national landmark to tell the historic Pilgrim story to a modern audience in a fresh, visually compelling way. When *Forefathers Monument Guidebook* was released in 2021, we were stunned by the response. Our first print run sold out in less than six months, and today, the *Guidebook* is currently in its third printing. In a world of revisionist history, people were hungry to read the truth about America's roots. The inspiring story of the Pilgrims was resonating across the nation. God knew.

I live in Plymouth, Massachusetts, not far from where the Forefathers Monument is located. It's a popular place for residents to walk and visit — especially for those of us in the faith community. It's a frequent site for our National Day of Prayer observance here in Plymouth, and many believers trek up to the monument throughout the year to be inspired, walk, and pray. In fact, that's exactly where I was when I had the inspiration to create *Monumental Prayers.* A crusade was coming to Plymouth, and a small group of intercessors had committed to pray for the event in the weeks leading up to it. We met every Saturday at the entrance to the Forefathers Monument. Walking the circular path around it together, we prayed aloud for the crusade organizers and asked God to send fresh winds of revival to Plymouth.

As I stood with the other intercessors one Saturday to pray, I looked up and it occurred to me: *You could literally just pray the monument.* So, we did. Walking around the circular path that afternoon, we took our prayer cues from the 81-foot-tall statue before us. We prayed for a revival of faith in our nation; we prayed for biblical morality; we prayed for righteous laws and leadership, for God's justice and mercy; we prayed for our youth and families, for wise parents and educators to guide our children in truth; we asked God to protect our liberty to worship Him freely and openly share the gospel. As I drove home from the prayer gathering that day, the idea for *Monumental Prayers* was born, and we published it the following year. It has been my deep honor to partner with Intercessors for America (IFA) and release this special edition of *Monumental Prayers* in celebration of IFA's 50th anniversary in 2023. I pray it blesses you.

Viewed as intended by the artist, the Forefathers Monument depicts the Pilgrim legacy in what is often called the "matrix of liberty." We come into a personal relationship with God through **Faith** in Jesus Christ. We receive **Morality** through the Bible, God's expressed will for our lives. Morality forms the basis for **Law.** God's laws are transmitted down through the generations by **Education,** which secures our God-given **Liberty.** *Faith* towers over the seated figures below her as the foundation for civic and religious freedom; remove any one of these elements, and *Liberty* fails. The *Forefathers Monument Guidebook* explores the deep symbolism of these five granite figures and their corresponding lower reliefs. They all testify to the Pilgrim legacy of faith and freedom and challenge every generation to "stand at the crossroads and look; ask for the ancient paths, ask where the good way is, and walk in it" (Jeremiah 6:16).

Each day of this 14-day devotional begins with a reflection on the historic Pilgrim legacy before moving into a five-point prayer focus guided by Scripture, with prompts to inspire your prayers:

1. Prayer of **Worship** *(Begin with adoration)*
2. Prayer of **Confession** *(Confess your sins and be forgiven)*
3. Prayer of **Petition** *(Pray for personal needs and concerns)*
4. Prayer of **Intercession** *(Pray for others)*
5. Prayer of **Thanksgiving** *(Conclude with gratitude)*

Acts 13:36 tells us that David *"served God's purpose in his own generation."* As you reflect on the Pilgrim story and meditate on God's word, I hope you will be inspired to serve God's purpose for your life in this generation. Like the early Pilgrims, we are merely sojourners here on earth; our true citizenship is in heaven. May we all – *through our own acts of faith and courage* – run the race that God has marked out before us with perseverance. "For we are God's handiwork, created in Christ Jesus to do good works, which God prepared in advance for us to do" (Ephesians 2:10).

For His glory,

Michelle Gallagher, author of the
Forefathers Monument Guidebook

"The *Pilgrims*: a simple people, inspired by an ardent *faith* in God, a *dauntless* courage in danger, a boundless *resourcefulness* in the face of difficulties, and impregnable *fortitude* in adversity; thus they have in some *measure* become the *spiritual* ancestors of all *Americans*."

- Samuel Eliot Morison, author, historian, Harvard professor and editor of William Bradford's *Of Plimoth Plantation*

Looking out from behind the Forefathers Monument reveals panoramic views of Plymouth's historic harbor. At right, the figure of *Faith* is shown facing east toward England, where the Pilgrims began their journey to America.

Table of Contents:

"May this monument

... as it shall stand here by day and by night, in storm and in sunshine, speak of devotion to truth and fidelity to conviction. May it prove a beacon to warn against the approach of the spirit of despotism, civil or religious, and an encouragement to devotion, to truth and right. Let it inspire all whose eyes shall rest upon it, now and hereafter, with a hatred of tyranny and a love of freedom and peace, a desire for that wisdom which is the product of education, a respect for law tempered by justice and mercy, and a reverence for morality and religion. May it help us and succeeding generations to treasure and transmit the rich legacy of civil and religious liberty bequeathed to us by the Pilgrim Fathers. *Amen.*"

- Invocation by the Grand Chaplain
  at the Dedication Ceremony, August 1, 1889

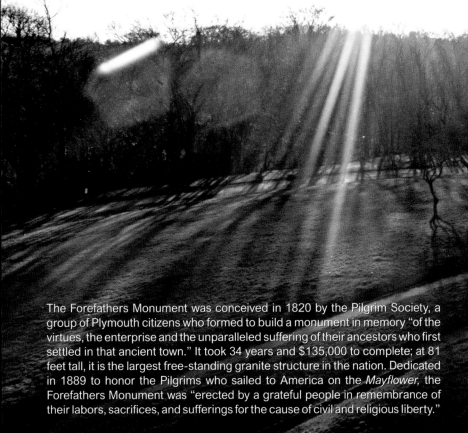

The Forefathers Monument was conceived in 1820 by the Pilgrim Society, a group of Plymouth citizens who formed to build a monument in memory "of the virtues, the enterprise and the unparalleled suffering of their ancestors who first settled in that ancient town." It took 34 years and $135,000 to complete; at 81 feet tall, it is the largest free-standing granite structure in the nation. Dedicated in 1889 to honor the Pilgrims who sailed to America on the *Mayflower*, the Forefathers Monument was "erected by a grateful people in remembrance of their labors, sacrifices, and sufferings for the cause of civil and religious liberty."

The Pilgrims emerged in England in the late 16th century, when the institutions of church and government were inexorably linked. By 1558, England's Act of Uniformity required all citizens to worship in the Church of England, regardless of their personal beliefs – or face a stiff penalty. *The Book of Common Prayer* was the only church liturgy approved by the state, and any worship services conducted apart from it were illegal. Those who disobeyed the rules were branded "nonconformists" and were considered traitors to the Crown. Religious acts of "heresy" were swiftly prosecuted by the state, and some violations were punishable by death.

The Pilgrims were known as Separatists: a group of devout Christians who believed the Church of England had been irrevocably corrupted by political interference and unbiblical, man-made rules. Choosing to separate from the Church of England rather than compromise their beliefs, these humble, law-abiding Christians were transformed into criminals and social outcasts overnight. Hiding out in the English countryside to evade the authorities, many were betrayed and exposed by their closest family members and friends. Arrested as traitors and enemies of the state, many Separatists were thrown into London's cold, disease-filled prisons, or publicly hanged.

Despite overwhelming pressure to comply – to relent and abide by the rules of the church – the Pilgrims refused to back down. Holding fast to their convictions even under threat to their very lives, the Pilgrims were committed to "walk in all His ways … whatever it should cost them, the Lord assisting them."[1] When England's persecution became more than they could bear, the Pilgrims still refused to abandon their faith; instead, they chose to leave. Fleeing England for Holland, the Pilgrims were finally free to gather and worship openly as a church and to "be ruled by the laws of God's word."[2]

But this freedom came at a price. After a decade of living together in the city of Leiden as a congregation, the heavy physical labor, secular Dutch culture, and fading influence of their own English heritage had taken a toll. The Pilgrims agonized over how to preserve their faith for future generations. Failing that, every other sacrifice would be in vain. They decided to leave Holland. For those Pilgrims who first set sail for America, there was no way to foresee the dangers ahead – or to know if they would even survive the journey across the Atlantic. Others had attempted the voyage before, with disastrous results. Despite the risks, the Pilgrims forged ahead in faith, believing of the trials that "all of them, through the help of God, by fortitude and patience, might either be borne or overcome."[3]

The Pilgrims spent over two months at sea onboard the *Mayflower,* cramped below deck in dark, foul-smelling quarters as the ship lurched and heaved through violent storms. When the ship finally reached land, it was late December. The passengers were weak and malnourished from their arduous journey across the Atlantic. Going ashore in frigid weather to build shelters on land, it wasn't long before many became deathly ill. Of the *Mayflower's* original 102 passengers, only 51 survived the first winter at Plymouth. For such a small group of people, the devastating impact of these losses is difficult to comprehend.

During that first winter at Plymouth, it was common for two or three people to die in a single day. Four entire families were wiped out completely. After surviving their treacherous voyage over a "vast and furious ocean," over a dozen men lost their wives to sickness after they safely reached land.[4] And yet, despite their trials and unspeakable grief, the Pilgrims never gave in to bitterness. Instead, they praised God for their deliverance. By spring, when most of their sick had finally recovered, William Bradford reflected that they had "borne their sad afflictions with as much patience and contentedness as I think any people could do. But it was the Lord who upheld them."[5]

At each pivotal moment in their story, the Pilgrims were determined to live – *and even to die, if the Lord allowed it* – according to the convictions of their faith. They believed that God had led them to plant their settlement at Plymouth Colony, and that from these small beginnings, the light of the Gospel could pierce a nation.

"The colonial dreamers agreed, believing the Sovereign was, indeed, birthing *'a city [nation] set on a hill that can't be hidden … a light to the world'* (Matthew 5:14). The Founders knew about the planting of the cross at Cape Henry in 1607, and the ensuing prayer meeting dedicating the land to God's glory. They had read the Mayflower Compact of 1620, stating the voyage was made 'for the glory of God, and advancement of the Christian faith.' The Founding Fathers absolutely believed America had a God-given destiny."[6] Faith would plant the seeds of freedom in America, and shining the light of the Gospel would become her divine destiny.

"If no *place* upon the face of the earth
should be free *for* us... we have a most
assured hope, that *heaven* itself is open
for us by *Christ,* who is the way."

- William Bradford

❶ PRAYER OF *Worship*

Glorify the Lord with me; let us exalt his name together. The righteous cry out, and the Lord hears them; he delivers them from all their troubles. The Lord is close to the brokenhearted and saves those who are crushed in spirit. (Psalm 34:3, 17-18)

God is our refuge and strength, an ever-present help in trouble. Therefore we will not fear, though the earth give way and the mountains fall into the heart of the sea, He says, "Be still, and know that I am God; I will be exalted among the nations, I will be exalted in the earth." (Psalm 46:1-2, 10)

The Pilgrim legacy of faith is a remarkable example of trusting God through every trial and circumstance of life. Reflect on how the Lord has responded to your own cries for help, and thank Him for His salvation and deliverance.

❷ PRAYER OF *Confession*

When my heart was grieved and my spirit embittered, I was senseless and ignorant; I was a brute beast before you. Yet I am always with you; you hold me by my right hand. You guide me with your counsel, and afterward you will take me into glory. Whom have I in heaven but you? And earth has nothing I desire besides you. My flesh and my heart may fail, but God is the strength of my heart and my portion forever. (Psalm 73:21-26)

Let us draw near to God with a sincere heart and with the full assurance that faith brings, having our hearts sprinkled to cleanse us from a guilty conscience. (Hebrews 10:22)

Repent, then, and turn to God, so that your sins may be wiped out, that times of refreshing may come from the Lord. (Acts 3:19)

Despite seasons of intense suffering and hardship, the Pilgrims refused to give in to bitterness; instead, they sought God through fasting, prayer, and worship. Ask the Holy Spirit to show you any hidden areas of sin in your own life. Draw near to God with a sincere heart of repentance, and be cleansed and refreshed in the Lord.

③ PRAYER OF *Petition*

I am not saying this because I am in need, for I have learned to be content whatever the circumstances. I know what it is to be in need, and I know what it is to have plenty. I have learned the secret of being content in any and every situation, whether well fed or hungry, whether living in plenty or in want. I can do all this through him who gives me strength. (Philippians 4:11-13)

Therefore I tell you, do not worry about your life, what you will eat or drink; or about your body, what you will wear. Is not life more than food, and the body more than clothes? Look at the birds of the air; they do not sow or reap or store away in barns, and yet your heavenly Father feeds them. Are you not much more valuable than they? (Matthew 6:25-26)

Remember those earlier days after you had received the light, when you endured in a great conflict full of suffering. Sometimes you were publicly exposed to insult and persecution; at other times you stood side by side with those who were so treated. You suffered along with those in prison and joyfully accepted the confiscation of your property, because you knew that you yourselves had better and lasting possessions. So do not throw away your confidence; it will be richly rewarded. You need to persevere so that when you have done the will of God, you will receive what he has promised. For, "In just a little while, he who is coming will come and will not delay." And, "But my righteous one will live by faith. And I take no pleasure in the one who shrinks back." (Hebrews 10:32-38)

May the God who gives endurance and encouragement give you the same attitude of mind toward each other that Christ Jesus had, so that with one mind and one voice you may glorify the God and Father of our Lord Jesus Christ. May the God of hope fill you with all joy and peace as you trust in him, so that you may overflow with hope by the power of the Holy Spirit. (Romans 15:5-6, 13)

As you reflect on how the Pilgrims endured hardships and affliction with patience and contentment, ask God to help you grow in your own faith. If you struggle with trusting God during times of uncertainty or lack, meditate on Jesus's Sermon on the Mount. Pray to your heavenly Father, who gives endurance and encouragement. Ask the Holy Spirit to show you how to persevere and live by faith, so you can do the will of God and please Him.

④ PRAYER OF *Intercession*

How good and pleasant it is when God's people live together in unity! (Psalm 133:1)

We remember before our God and Father your work produced by faith, your labor prompted by love, and your endurance inspired by hope in our Lord Jesus Christ. (1 Thessalonians 1:3)

For I am not ashamed of the gospel, because it is the power of God that brings salvation to everyone who believes: first to the Jew, then to the Gentile. For in the gospel the righteousness of God is revealed—a righteousness that is by faith from first to last, just as it is written: "The righteous will live by faith." (Romans 1:16-18)

Pray for the local churches in your area, especially for your own pastors, elders, leaders, and their families. Pray for a spirit of unity among all believers, and a genuine display of labor prompted by love. Intercede for those in your life who have not yet placed their faith in Jesus; call them out by name and ask God to give them a holy visitation. Ask the Holy Spirit for opportunities and boldness to share your testimony of how Christ changed your life.

⑤ PRAYER OF *Thanksgiving*

I keep asking that the God of our Lord Jesus Christ, the glorious Father, may give you the Spirit of wisdom and revelation, so that you may know him better. I pray that the eyes of your heart may be enlightened in order that you may know the hope to which he has called you... and his incomparably great power for us who believe. (Ephesians 1:17-19)

Now to him who is able to do immeasurably more than all we ask or imagine, according to his power that is at work within us, to him be glory in the church and in Christ Jesus throughout all generations, for ever and ever! Amen. (Ephesians 3:20-21)

As the Pilgrims studied God's Word for themselves, they experienced a spiritual transformation that changed their lives forever. Ask the Holy Spirit to give you wisdom and revelation. Thank God for your eternal salvation, and for the glorious inheritance that awaits all who trust in Jesus Christ.

Do not be *anxious* about anything, but in every situation, by prayer and *petition,* with *thanksgiving,* present your requests to God. And the peace of God, *which* transcends all *understanding,* will guard your hearts and *your* minds in *Christ* Jesus.

(Philippians 4:6-7)

JUSTICE

MORALITY

24

In 1798, President John Adams, noted signer of the Declaration of Independence, said of America: "We have no government armed with power capable of contending with human passions unbridled by morality and religion… our Constitution was made only for a moral and religious people. It is wholly inadequate to the government of any other."[7]

Morality represents a vital aspect of the Pilgrim legacy—as well as a fundamental requirement necessary for self-government. But for the Pilgrims, morality was more than simply a set of rules to follow; it embodied the moral character and ethics on display in everyday life. The Pilgrims believed it was their duty to model the Christian virtues revealed in the Bible and taught in church.

Their pastor, John Robinson, cautioned against religious hypocrites: those who claimed to love God but failed to love their neighbor. He admonished his congregation that any displays of devotion to God in the church should be equally matched "in the house, and streets, with loving-kindness, and mercy and all goodness towards men."[8] The biblical command to "do to others as you would have them do to you" (Luke 6:31), would be evident throughout the Pilgrim story, even to those who persecuted them or ridiculed their faith.

By every reliable account, the Pilgrims were characterized as honest, hard-working, charitable, and kind. Although they arrived in Holland as immigrants and outsiders, the Pilgrims became highly regarded in their local communities. They lived peacefully together as a congregation in Leiden, and "if any differences arose or offences broke out – as cannot but be even amongst the best of men – they were always so met with and nipped in the head… [so] that love, peace, and communion continued."[9]

Although they were considered poor, the Dutch business owners came to know the Pilgrim's character and often extended them credit. Local neighborhood bakers and shopkeepers were known to "trust them to any reasonable extent when they lacked money to buy what they needed. They found by experience how careful they were to keep their word, and saw how diligent they were."[10] Dutch merchants competed heartily for the Pilgrim's business and often employed them in preference over others.

At Plymouth Colony, the Pilgrims were free to shape their new settlement according to the tenets of their faith. The Pilgrims were friendly and welcoming by nature, and William Bradford chronicled their desire to "show a rare example of brotherly love and Christian care" to all who later joined the colony.[11] As proof of this, "during the first three decades of Plymouth Colony, no stranger was turned away and the plantation endeavored to extend hospitality to those who came seeking a haven."[12]

The Pilgrims were devoted to sharing the gospel in word and deed. When Bradford chronicled the church's decision to leave Holland for a new start in America, he wrote: "Last and not least, they cherished a great hope and inward zeal of laying good foundations, or at least of making some way towards it, for the propagation and advance of the gospel of the kingdom of Christ in the remote parts of the world, even though they should be but stepping stones to others in the performance of so great a work."[13]

The Pilgrims pored over biblical examples of how God had used ordinary people to accomplish His divine purposes. Pinning their hope on God's infallible Word, they believed that through "his great and precious promises," they too could "participate in the divine nature" (2 Peter 1:3-4).

"More than 150 years passed before the descendants of New England's founders finally united with the other English colonists to challenge an empire and achieve independence. The passage of five generations meant profound changes in wealth, values, occupations, communication, political philosophy, and even theology among the thriving providences of eighteenth-century English America. But one characteristic consistently connected the Pilgrims of 1620 and the patriots of 1776: an unshakable conviction in their own significance as part of a divinely ordained design for their country."[14]

1 PRAYER OF *Worship*

Sing to the Lord a new song; sing to the Lord, all the earth. Sing to the Lord, praise his name; proclaim his salvation day after day. Declare his glory among the nations, his marvelous deeds among all peoples. For great is the Lord and most worthy of praise; he is to be feared above all gods. For all the gods of the nations are idols, but the Lord made the heavens. Splendor and majesty are before him; strength and glory are in his sanctuary. Worship the Lord in the splendor of his holiness; tremble before him, all the earth. (Psalm 96:1-6, 9)

Pause to contemplate the splendor and majesty of Almighty God, who is most worthy of our praise. Speaking from your own heart, thank Him for the joy of your salvation and for God's marvelous deeds in your life.

2 PRAYER OF *Confession*

Pride goes before destruction, a haughty spirit before a fall. (Proverbs 16:18)

Bless those who persecute you; bless and do not curse them. Repay no one evil for evil, but give thought to do what is honorable in the sight of all. (Romans 12:14, 17)

Then I acknowledged my sin to you and did not cover up my iniquity. I said, "I will confess my transgressions to the Lord." And you forgave the guilt of my sin. Therefore let all the faithful pray to you while you may be found. (Psalm 32:5-6)

The Pilgrims were known for their Christian conduct of love, compassion, and mercy; even blessing those who persecuted them. Pause for a moment to reflect with humility on your own reputation as a Christian. Ask the Lord to show you areas where you may have fallen short, or pride has taken root. Acknowledge your sins to God, and ask Him to renew your heart and Christian witness.

❸ PRAYER OF *Petition*

I am the vine; you are the branches. Whoever abides in me and I in him, he it is that bears much fruit, for apart from me you can do nothing. (John 15:5)

Love must be sincere. Hate what is evil; cling to what is good. Be devoted to one another in love. Honor one another above yourselves. Never be lacking in zeal, but keep your spiritual fervor, serving the Lord. Be joyful in hope, patient in affliction, faithful in prayer. (Romans 12:9-12)

Therefore, I urge you, brothers and sisters, in view of God's mercy, to offer your bodies as a living sacrifice, holy and pleasing to God–this is your true and proper worship. Do not conform to the pattern of this world, but be transformed by the renewing of your mind. Then you will be able to test and approve what God's will is–his good, pleasing and perfect will. (Romans 12:1-2)

But the fruit of the Spirit is love, joy, peace, forbearance, kindness, goodness, faithfulness, gentleness and self-control. Against such things there is no law. (Galatians 5:22)

Those who live according to the flesh have their minds set on what the flesh desires; but those who live in accordance with the Spirit have their minds set on what the Spirit desires. For if you live according to the flesh, you will die; but if by the Spirit you put to death the misdeeds of the body, you will live. For those who are led by the Spirit of God are the children of God. (Romans 8:5, 13-14)

As you reflect on the Pilgrim's legacy of high moral character, ask God to help you demonstrate the fruit of the Spirit in your life — personally, professionally, and spiritually — and in your conduct with others. Determine to renew your mind daily with God's Word. Ask God to help you die to your flesh and live according to the Spirit, so you can abide in Christ and bear much fruit.

④ PRAYER OF *Intercession*

Do not love the world or anything in the world. If anyone loves the world, love for the Father is not in them. For everything in the world— the lust of the flesh, the lust of the eyes, and the pride of life—comes not from the Father but from the world. (1 John 2:15-16)

That, however, is not the way of life you learned when you heard about Christ... You were taught, with regard to your former way of life, to put off your old self, which is being corrupted by its deceitful desires; to be made new in the attitude of your minds; and to put on the new self, created to be like God in true righteousness and holiness. (Ephesians 4:20-24)

Or do you show contempt for the riches of his kindness, forbearance and patience, not realizing that God's kindness is intended to lead you to repentance? (Romans 2:4)

The end of all things is near. Therefore be alert and of sober mind so that you may pray. Above all, love each other deeply, because love covers over a multitude of sins. If you are insulted because of the name of Christ, you are blessed, for the Spirit of glory and of God rests on you. If you suffer, it should not be as a murderer or thief or any other kind of criminal, or even as a meddler. However, if you suffer as a Christian, do not be ashamed, but praise God that you bear that name. For it is time for judgment to begin with God's household; and if it begins with us, what will the outcome be for those who do not obey the gospel of God? (1 Peter 4:7-8, 15-17)

Follow God's example, therefore, as dearly loved children and walk in the way of love, just as Christ loved us and gave himself up for us as a fragrant offering and sacrifice to God. For you were once darkness, but now you are light in the Lord. Live as children of light. (Ephesians 5:1-2, 8)

The Pilgrims were a powerful example of how to operate in biblical love and holiness as a congregation. Pray for the Body of Christ, that our local churches would be united, and devoted to one another in love and prayer. Intercede for those in the church who are ensnared by sin, that God's kindness would lead to sincere repentance. Pray that God's children would live as children of light and display God's glory for the world to see.

⑤ PRAYER OF *Thanksgiving*

The Lord upholds all who fall, and lifts up all who are bowed down. The Lord is near to all who call on him, to all who call on him in truth. He fulfills the desires of those who fear him; he hears their cry and saves them. (Psalm 145:14, 18-19)

He will also keep you firm to the end, so that you will be blameless on the day of our Lord Jesus Christ. God is faithful, who has called you into fellowship with his Son, Jesus Christ our Lord. (1 Corinthians 1:8-9)

Meditate on God's faithfulness and offer your own prayers of thanksgiving.

BELOW: The front dedication panel of the Forefathers Monument in Plymouth, Massachusetts.

Evangelist

On the right of *Morality's* pedestal, the Pilgrims' zeal for evangelism is represented by the figure of the *Evangelist*. In the New Testament, Jesus issued the Great Commission to his followers, declaring: "Therefore go and make disciples of all nations, baptizing them in the name of the Father and of the Son and of the Holy Spirit, and teaching them to obey everything I have commanded you. And surely I am with you always, to the very end of the age" (Matthew 28:19-20).

The Pilgrims received God's word as their final authority in all matters, and they took their commission seriously as believers to spread the gospel. It was their obedience to God's word that first drove them to risk their lives by leaving the Church of England. Their pastor, John Robinson, wrote, "The profit and power of the Scriptures, both for stay of faith, and rule of life, and comfort in all manner of afflictions, no tongue or pen is able so fully to express, as every true Christian finds, and feels, in his own experience. There is but one true happiness, life eternal; one giver of it, God; one Mediator, Jesus Christ; and so but one means of imparting it, the word of God."[15]

The Pilgrims measured their faithfulness as Christians according to their willingness to obey God's Word. "The holy Scriptures," taught Robinson, "are that Divine instrument, and means, by which we are taught to believe what we ought, touching God, and ourselves, and all creatures, and how to please God in all things, unto eternal life."[16] When the Pilgrims were forced to follow unbiblical rules in church worship, they refused. Rather than disobey Scripture, they eventually left their homes in the English countryside to live as exiles in Holland.

But when life in Leiden became unsustainable, William Bradford recorded their reasons for choosing to make a fresh start in America. Bradford wrote: "Last and not least, they cherished a great hope and inward zeal of laying good foundations, or at least of making some way towards it, for the propagation and advance of the gospel of the kingdom of Christ in the remote parts of the world, even though they should be but stepping stones to others in the performance of so great a work."[17]

The Geneva Bible arrived in America on the *Mayflower,* and along with it, the gospel of Jesus Christ. The Pilgrims were eager to share their faith with the native population, and Bradford recorded the

ABOVE: The *Evangelist* holds a quill pen and an open book, poised to record new names in the Lamb's Book of Life.

occasion of leading Squanto to faith in Christ before his untimely death so "he might go to the Englishmen's God in heaven."[18] The first Bible printed in America wasn't created for the colonists, but for the native population.

In 1653, a Puritan minister named John Eliot hoped to better evangelize the native population in Massachusetts Bay by presenting the gospel in their native tongue. For eight painstaking years, Eliot worked with linguists and translators to produce a translation of the Geneva Bible in an Algonquian language called Natick. In time, there would be towns filled with natives who had converted to Christianity in communities known as "praying Indians." Despite the many failures, conflicts, and injustices that accompanied the colonization of New England after the Pilgrims landed, the gospel would advance.

In 1734, a young preacher named Jonathan Edwards led a revival in Northampton, Massachusetts, igniting the First Great Awakening. In just six months, 300 souls were converted in a town of only 1,100 people. In 1739, George Whitefield carried the torch of revival in Philadelphia, and hundreds of thousands of colonists flocked to hear him preach. In 1831, Charles Finney saw 100,000 people converted in Rochester, New York, alone – spreading revival to 1,500 towns nearby. In 1857, Dwight L. Moody led revivals in Chicago and America's biggest cities, and hundreds of thousands of souls were converted. In 1904, the Welsh Revival spread like wildfire across Pennsylvania, bringing 1 million souls to Christ.

Azuza Street. Campus Crusade for Christ. The Gideons. Billy Graham Crusades. The Jesus Movement. Promise Keepers. From the creation of the first Indian Bible in America to revivals that have stirred each generation since, the Pilgrims' hope of being a stepping stone to advance God's kingdom on earth would be realized beyond their wildest dreams.

1 PRAYER OF *Worship*

Praise the Lord. I will extol the Lord with all my heart in the council of the upright and in the assembly. Great are the works of the Lord; they are pondered by all who delight in them. Glorious and majestic are his deeds, and his righteousness endures forever. He has caused his wonders to be remembered; the Lord is gracious and compassionate. He provides food for those who fear him; he remembers his covenant forever. (Psalm 111:1-5)

When I am afraid, I put my trust in you. In God, whose word I praise, in the Lord, whose word I praise—in God I trust and am not afraid. What can man do to me? I am under vows to you, my God; I will present my thank offerings to you. For you have delivered me from death and my feet from stumbling, that I may walk before God in the light of life. (Psalm 56:3, 10-13)

Present your thank offerings to Almighty God, who has delivered you from death, and is gracious and compassionate toward you.

2 PRAYER OF *Confession*

Then I acknowledged my sin to you and did not cover up my iniquity. I said, "I will confess my transgressions to the Lord." And you forgave the guilt of my sin. (Psalm 32:5)

Whoever acknowledges me before others, I will also acknowledge before my Father in heaven. But whoever disowns me before others, I will disown before my Father in heaven. (Matthew 10:32-33)

Ask the Lord to search your heart. Repent for moments when you have grieved the Holy Spirit by failing to acknowledge Jesus Christ before others. Ask God to create in you a clean heart and give you a bold witness. Thank God for His infinite mercy and forgiveness.

3 PRAYER OF *Petition*

Always be prepared to give an answer to everyone who asks you to give the reason for the hope that you have. But do this with gentleness and respect, keeping a clear conscience, so that those who speak maliciously against your good behavior in Christ may be ashamed of their slander. (1 Peter 3:15-16)

I give you this charge: Preach the word; be prepared in season and out of season; correct, rebuke and encourage – with great patience and careful instruction. For the time will come when people will not put up with sound doctrine... They will turn their ears away from the truth and turn aside to myths. But you, keep your head in all situations, endure hardship, do the work of an evangelist, discharge all the duties of your ministry. (2 Timothy 4:1-5)

Ask God to give you His heart, the heart of an evangelist. If you have never been comfortable talking about Jesus with others, be honest. Ask the Holy Spirit to help you. Discipline yourself to study the Bible so you can be ready with a word of hope or encouragement when opportunities arise to share the gospel. Ask for the courage to speak when God prompts you to share your testimony with others.

4 PRAYER OF *Intercession*

How, then, can they call on the one they have not believed in? And how can they believe in the one of whom they have not heard? And how can they hear without someone preaching to them? And how can anyone preach unless they are sent? As it is written: "How beautiful are the feet of those who bring good news!" (Romans 10: 14-15)

Intercede for our nation. Ask God to raise up a bold army of messengers who will proclaim Christ to a generation without hope in this hour. Decree Romans 5:20 over our nation: where evil abounds, God's grace will abound even greater! Declare our nation's covenant with Almighty God: America was created for the glory of God and the advancement of the Christian faith. Pray for a spirit of holiness and repentance to sweep our nation, especially among our leaders. Ask God to ignite fresh fires of spiritual awakening for our generation.

⑤ PRAYER OF *Thanksgiving*

I will remember the deeds of the Lord; yes, I will remember your miracles of long ago. I will consider all your works and meditate on all your mighty deeds. Your ways, God, are holy. What god is as great as our God? You are the God who performs miracles; you display your power among the peoples. With your mighty arm you redeemed your people, the descendants of Jacob and Joseph. (Psalm 77:11-15)

Meditate on the Lord's great deeds in your life, and in the life of this nation. Thank God for the privilege of living in America, and for our great legacy of civil and religious freedom. Declare your faith in the God who performs miracles! Thank Him for redeeming you, your loved ones, and this nation for His glory.

BELOW: Underneath the figure of *Morality*, a marble relief panel entitled *Embarkation* depicts the scene of the Pilgrims leaving Holland for their voyage to America.

PROPHET

To the left of *Morality's* pedestal is the *Prophet,* one who speaks a divine message on behalf of God Almighty in the manner of the Old Testament prophet Amos, who declared: "Surely the Sovereign Lord does nothing without revealing his plan to his servants the prophets" (Amos 3:7).

The Pilgrims were inspired by Bible accounts of God choosing ordinary and even flawed people to accomplish His plans on earth – and they prayed that they, too, might be used for divine ends. Before God brought judgment on the earth in the form of a flood, He chose Noah to rescue a remnant of His creation. Before God delivered the Israelites out of slavery in Egypt, He chose Moses to be a leader over his people. When Jesus called the disciples, He chose 12 ordinary men and charged them to "heal the sick, raise the dead, cleanse those who have leprosy, drive out demons," adding that "whoever welcomes a prophet as a prophet will receive a prophet's reward" (Matthew 10:8, 41).

Each member of the Pilgrim congregation entered into a sacred covenant before joining the church. "These reformers who saw the evil of these things, and whose hearts the Lord had touched with heavenly zeal for His truth, shook off this yoke of anti-Christian bondage and as the Lord's free people joined themselves together by covenant as a church, in the fellowship of the gospel to walk in all His ways, made known, or to be made known to them, according to their best endeavors, whatever it should cost them, the Lord assisting them."[19]

As brothers and sisters in Christ, the Pilgrims swore a sacred covenant oath to walk in all of God's ways, no matter the cost, and prayed their example would point others to Christ. Indeed, it did. "For by these so public troubles, in so many eminent places, their cause became famous, and occasioned many to look into the same; and their Godly carriage and Christian behavior was such as left a deep impression in the minds of many."[20]

History records the impact of the Pilgrims' testimony and how God used this humble group of devout Christians to lay the foundation for biblical faith and freedom in America. Two decades after the Pilgrims established Plymouth Colony, new settlements had spread

ABOVE: The *Prophet* is shown holding the Decalogue and lifting his hand toward God in heaven.

throughout the region. This growth led to an alliance known as the United Colonies of New England, joining four Puritan colonies in Massachusetts, Connecticut, New Haven, and Plymouth. This alliance would be one of many future efforts to unify the expanding colonies on America's path to independence.

On May 19, 1643, the Articles of Confederation for the United Colonies of New England indicated the desire of early believers to be a voice for God in the New World:

"Whereas we all came into these parts of America with one and the same end and aim, namely, to advance the Kingdom of our Lord Jesus Christ and to enjoy the liberties of the Gospel in purity with peace; and whereas in our settling (by a wise Providence of God) we are further dispersed upon the sea coasts and rivers than was at first intended, so that we can not according to our desire with convenience communicate... We therefore do conceive it our bound duty, without delay to enter into a present Consociation among ourselves, for mutual help and strength… [and] enter into a firm and perpetual league of friendship and amity for… defense, mutual advice and... for preserving and propagating the truth and liberties of the Gospel and for their own mutual safety and welfare."[21]

The impact of these early believers as God's prophetic voice in government is profound. From New York's gratitude *"to Almighty God for our freedom,"* to Connecticut's free *"enjoyment of religious profession and worship,"* to Maryland's *"pious Zeal for extending the Christian Religion,"* and Delaware's *"propagation of the Holy Gospel"* – each of the original 13 colonies would acknowledge God as their divine source of liberty and cement freedom of religious expression in their constitutions and colonial charters. The prophet Isaiah declared that government would rest on Jesus' shoulders. Throughout America's history, Christians would take up the mantle of the prophet to boldly speak God's message to a nation.

❶ PRAYER OF *Worship*

For thus says the One who is high and lifted up, who inhabits eternity, whose name is Holy: "I dwell in the high and holy place, and also with him who is of a contrite and lowly spirit, to revive the spirit of the lowly, and to revive the heart of the contrite." (Isaiah 57:15)

The Lord is my strength and my shield; in him my heart trusts, and I am helped; my heart exults, and with my song I give thanks to him. The Lord is the strength of his people; he is the saving refuge of his anointed. (Psalm 28:7-8)

Praise the Almighty God in heaven who inhabits eternity. In your own words, praise God for being a saving refuge in your life and an eternal source of strength.

❷ PRAYER OF *Confession*

To the Lord our God belong mercy and forgiveness, for we have rebelled against him and have not obeyed the voice of the Lord our God by walking in his laws, which he set before us by his servants the prophets. O my God, incline your ear and hear... we do not present our pleas before you because of our righteousness, but because of your great mercy. O Lord, forgive." (Daniel 9:9-10,18-19)

Come before the Lord with a heart of repentance, and receive forgiveness through Jesus Christ, the righteous Lamb of God.

❸ PRAYER OF *Petition*

As you come to him, a living stone rejected by men but in the sight of God chosen and precious, you yourselves like living stones are being built up as a spiritual house, to be a holy priesthood, to offer spiritual sacrifices acceptable to God through Jesus Christ. But you are a chosen race, a royal priesthood, a holy nation, a people for his own possession, that you may proclaim the excellencies of him who called you out of darkness into his marvelous light. (1 Peter 2:4-5,9)

"Whoever loves his life loses it, and whoever hates his life in this world will keep it for eternal life. If anyone serves me, he must follow me; and where I am, there will my servant be also. If anyone serves me, the Father will honor him." (John 12:25-26)

The word of the Lord came to Jeremiah a second time, while he was still shut up in the court of the guard: "Thus says the Lord who made the earth, the Lord who formed it to establish it—the Lord is his name: Call to me and I will answer you, and will tell you great and hidden things that you have not known." (Jeremiah 33:1-4)

The Pilgrims understood their calling as God's people to proclaim and serve the will of God before the world. Ask the Lord to show you how He wants to use your voice in this hour. Pray for a heart that is fully surrendered to Christ. Ask the Holy Spirit for divine revelation concerning your calling to proclaim and serve the will of God in your lifetime.

❹ PRAYER OF *Intercession*

The Spirit of the Sovereign Lord is on me, because the Lord has anointed me to proclaim good news to the poor. He has sent me to bind up the brokenhearted, to proclaim freedom for the captives and release from darkness for the prisoners, to proclaim the year of the Lord's favor and the day of vengeance of our God. (Isaiah 61:1-2)

And it shall come to pass afterward, that I will pour out my Spirit on all flesh; your sons and your daughters shall prophesy, your old men shall dream dreams, and your young men shall see visions. Even on the male and female servants in those days I will pour out my Spirit. (Joel 2:28-29)

See to it that no one takes you captive through hollow and deceptive philosophy, which depends on human tradition and the elemental spiritual forces of this world rather than on Christ. (Colossians 2:8)

So Paul and Barnabas spent considerable time there, speaking boldly for the Lord, who confirmed the message of his grace by enabling them to perform signs and wonders. (Acts 14:3)

Pray for courageous voices who will boldly speak God's truth in this hour. Ask God to raise up leaders in every area of society — in politics, education, media, and popular culture — as His messengers to a lost generation. Pray for church leaders who will unapologetically proclaim the Bible as the full counsel of God's truth. Pray for a prophetic move of Almighty God that will sweep through our churches and spill out onto the streets. Ask for a supernatural increase in signs and wonders to confirm God's message of grace and liberate those held captive by spiritual darkness.

⑤ PRAYER OF *Thanksgiving*

In God, whose word I praise, in the Lord, whose word I praise, in God I trust; I shall not be afraid. What can man do to me? I must perform my vows to you, O God; I will render thank offerings to you. For you have delivered my soul from death, yes, my feet from falling, that I may walk before God in the light of life. (Psalm 56:10-13)

Offer your own thoughts of thanksgiving to God, who has delivered you from death to walk before Him in the light of life.

BELOW: The remains of those who died that first winter at Plymouth Colony are memorialized in a Sarcophagus located on Cole's Hill in Plymouth, overlooking the historic waterfront.

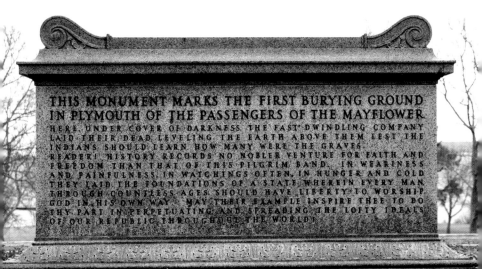

THIS MONUMENT MARKS THE FIRST BURYING GROUND IN PLYMOUTH OF THE PASSENGERS OF THE MAYFLOWER HERE UNDER COVER OF DARKNESS THE FAST DWINDLING COMPANY LAID THEIR DEAD LEVELING THE EARTH ABOVE THEM LEST THE INDIANS SHOULD LEARN HOW MANY WERE THE GRAVES READER! HISTORY RECORDS NO NOBLER VENTURE FOR FAITH AND FREEDOM THAN THAT OF THIS PILGRIM BAND. IN WEARINESS AND PAINFULNESS IN WATCHINGS OFTEN, IN HUNGER AND COLD THEY LAID THE FOUNDATIONS OF A STATE WHEREIN EVERY MAN THROUGH COUNTLESS AGES SHOULD HAVE LIBERTY TO WORSHIP GOD IN HIS OWN WAY MAY THEIR EXAMPLE INSPIRE THEE TO DO THY PART IN PERPETUATING AND SPREADING THE LOFTY IDEALS OF OUR REPUBLIC THROUGHOUT THE WORLD!

When the Mayflower sailed off course into the waters of Cape Cod, the Pilgrims found themselves well outside their legal jurisdiction. Their Virginia land patent had no effect in this new territory, and the only recognized authority was vested in Captain Christopher Jones onboard the ship. The Pilgrims considered abandoning their Virginia charter for a new life in Plymouth, but certain passengers who were not part of the Leiden congregation resisted the idea. Some even threatened to go off on their own after they reached land, claiming that no one had the power to stop them. They were right.

To solve this problem, the Pilgrims relied on their own history as a church congregation. From their first meetings in Scrooby, England, to their years together living as exiles in Leiden, the Pilgrims were governed independently as a congregation. Members freely "joined themselves together by covenant as a church," declaring a solemn oath to walk in all of God's ways.[22] As a church body, the congregation chose its own leaders, and even the decision to leave for America was decided by a majority vote. As their pastor, John Robinson, wrote: "We are knit together as a body in a most strict and sacred bond and covenant of the Lord, of the violation whereof we make great conscience, and by virtue whereof we hold ourselves straitly tied to all care of each other's good."[23]

For the rest of the passengers on the Mayflower, any concept of government was limited to their experience as subjects in the British monarchy. For these secular-minded merchants, workers, and adventurers, the idea of self-government was completely foreign. Despite being in the minority, the Pilgrims were the only passengers onboard with any experience in self-governance, so they went to work. Drafting a new agreement to replace their obsolete land patent, each signer freely swore an oath before God and each other; pledging to submit to all the duly elected leaders and laws of their new settlement, which would be enacted for the good of everyone. Sound familiar?

On November 11, 1620, the Mayflower Compact was signed by 41 men in the main cabin of the ship to represent every household in the new colony. Written in the language of biblical covenant, the document reveals the deep influence of faith in the new settlement that would come to be known as Plymouth Colony.

"In the name of God, Amen. We… having undertaken, for the Glory of God, and advancements of the and advancements of the Christian faith, and the honor of our King and Country… a voyage to plant the first colony in the Northern parts of Virginia… do by… solemnly and mutually, in the presence of God, and one another… covenant and combine ourselves together into a civil body politic."[24]

The Pilgrims recognized government as a function of God's earthly order, the authority of which rests on the Lord Jesus Christ. "For to us a child is born, to us a son is given, and the government will be on his shoulders… of the greatness of his government and peace there will be no end. He will reign… with justice and righteousness… the zeal of the Lord Almighty will accomplish this" (Isaiah 9:6-7). The Pilgrims were heavily influenced by prominent Reformers such as John Calvin and Martin Luther, who articulated the divine purpose of government as a civil mechanism to restrain man's sinful nature and create a peaceful society where all are free to worship God.

In letters to his departing congregation, Pastor Robinson reminded the Pilgrims of their sacred role as God's representatives in civil government and urged them to select their leaders wisely. "Lastly, whereas you are to become a body politic, administering among yourselves civil government, and are furnished with persons of no special eminence above the rest, from whom you will elect some to the office of government, let your wisdom and godliness appear, not only in choosing such persons as will entirely love and promote the common good, but also in yielding them all due honour and obedience in their lawful administrations; not beholding in them the ordinariness of their persons, but God's ordinance for your own good."[25]

At Plymouth Colony, the Pilgrims affirmed God's divine design for government by vowing to create "just and equal laws, ordinances, acts, constitutions, and offices" to serve the greater good of all.[26] They enacted the *Rule of Law* to ensure that all citizens were accountable to the same laws regardless of their power or position, a direct reflection that "with the Lord our God there is no injustice or partiality or bribery" (2 Chronicles 19:7). By working to establish biblical standards of morality and justice, the Pilgrims sought to fulfill their calling as Christians to "act justly and to love mercy and to walk humbly" as the Lord's servants in creating righteous laws and government (Micah 6:8).

"The religion which has introduced civil *liberty* is the religion of *Christ* and His apostles, which enjoins humility, piety, and benevolence; which *acknowledges* in every person a brother, or a sister, and a citizen with *equal* rights. This is genuine Christianity, and to this we owe our *free* Constitutions of Government."

- Noah Webster (1758-1843), American lexicographer, textbook pioneer, and considered the "Father of American Scholarship and Education"

① PRAYER OF *Worship*

In the beginning was the Word, and the Word was with God, and the Word was God. The Word became flesh and made his dwelling among us. We have seen his glory, the glory of the one and only Son, who came from the Father, full of grace and truth. (John 1:1,14)

Therefore, there is now no condemnation for those who are in Christ Jesus, because through Christ Jesus the law of the Spirit who gives life has set you free from the law of sin and death. (Romans 8:1-2)

Righteousness and justice are the foundation of your throne; love and faithfulness go before you. (Psalm 89:14)

Worship the Lord God Almighty, who revealed Himself to mankind through His one and only Son, Jesus, the Word made flesh. Praise God for His perfect plan of salvation, and for setting you free from the law of sin and death.

② PRAYER OF *Confession*

There are six things the Lord hates, seven that are detestable to him: haughty eyes, a lying tongue, hands that shed innocent blood, a heart that devises wicked schemes, feet that are quick to rush into evil, a false witness who pours out lies and a person who stirs up conflict in the community. (Proverbs 6:16-19)

Now Daniel so distinguished himself among the administrators and the satraps by his exceptional qualities that the king planned to set him over the whole kingdom. At this, the administrators and the satraps tried to find grounds for charges against Daniel in his conduct of government affairs, but they were unable to do so. They could find no corruption in him, because he was trustworthy and neither corrupt nor negligent. (Daniel 6:3-4)

Both Daniel and the Pilgrims lived in a way that set them apart from others in their lifetime, and were known for their integrity and diligence because of their walk with God. As you reflect on their example, ask the Holy Spirit to reveal any areas of hidden sin or compromise in your life. Ask God to help you conduct yourself in a way that glorifies Him in your daily interactions with others.

③ PRAYER OF *Petition*

Teach me, Lord, the way of your decrees, that I may follow it to the end. Give me understanding, so that I may keep your law and obey it with all my heart. Turn my eyes away from worthless things; preserve my life according to your word. (Psalm 119:33-34, 37)

Blessed is the one who does not walk in step with the wicked or stand in the way that sinners take or sit in the company of mockers, but whose delight is in the law of the Lord, and who meditates on his law day and night. That person is like a tree planted by streams of water, which yields its fruit in season and whose leaf does not wither— whatever they do prospers. (Psalm 1:1-3)

The Pilgrims relied on the Bible as the pattern for their own Christian walk, and to form laws that promoted freedom and justice at Plymouth Colony. As you meditate upon Scripture yourself, ask the Holy Spirit to give you wisdom and understanding — and a heart that delights in God's law. In times of increasing busyness and confusion, ask the Lord to help you turn your eyes away from worthless things and draw you into a deeper study of God's word as the anchor of your faith and biblical worldview.

④ PRAYER OF *Intercession*

The Lord foils the plans of the nations; he thwarts the purposes of the peoples. But the plans of the Lord stand firm forever, the purposes of his heart through all generations. Blessed is the nation whose God is the Lord, the people he chose for his inheritance. (Psalm 33:10-12)

Praise be to the name of God for ever and ever; wisdom and power are his. He changes times and seasons; he deposes kings and raises up others. He gives wisdom to the wise and knowledge to the discerning. (Daniel 2:20-21)

The fear of the Lord is the beginning of wisdom, and knowledge of the Holy One is understanding. For through wisdom your days will be many, and years will be added to your life. (Proverbs 9:10-11)

Righteousness exalts a nation, but sin condemns any people. (Proverbs 14:34)

If you fully obey the Lord your God and carefully follow all his commands I give you today, the Lord your God will set you high above all the nations on earth. (Deuteronomy 28:1)

I urge, then, first of all, that petitions, prayers, intercession and thanksgiving be made for all people – for kings and all those in authority, that we may live peaceful and quiet lives in all godliness and holiness. This is good, and pleases God our Savior, who wants all people to be saved and to come to a knowledge of the truth. (1 Timothy 2:1-4)

Pastor Robinson urged the Pilgrims to use wisdom and godliness when selecting leaders for their new colony. Commit to pray for your leaders, and ask God for wisdom when casting your vote. Ask God to visit our government officials at local, state, and national levels — up to the highest offices in the land. Pray for righteous laws to prevail, and for judges who will serve justice with wisdom and integrity. Ask the Lord to raise up civic leaders who fear God, not man. Ask the Lord to use those in authority to safeguard America's liberties, so we can freely share the gospel here and around the world.

5 PRAYER OF  *Thanksgiving*

"This is the covenant I will make with the people of Israel after that time," declares the Lord. "I will put my law in their minds and write it on their hearts. I will be their God, and they will be my people. (Jeremiah 31:33)

For the grace of God has appeared that offers salvation to all people. (Titus 2:11)

But you are a chosen people, a royal priesthood, a holy nation, God's special possession, that you may declare the praises of him who called you out of darkness into his wonderful light. (1 Peter 2:9)

Give thanks to Almighty God, who writes His laws on the hearts of His people. As the Lord's special possession, thank God for calling you out of darkness and setting you free in Christ.

Your *word,* Lord, is eternal; it stands firm in the *heavens.* Your laws *endure* to this day, for all things serve *you.*

(Psalm 119:89,91)

MERCY

For the Pilgrims, mercy was not merely a crucial balance for justice in the courtroom, but a personal mandate as followers of Christ: "Therefore, as God's chosen people, holy and dearly loved, clothe yourselves with compassion, kindness, humility, gentleness and patience" (Colossians 3:12). This charge was never more apparent than at the start of the Pilgrim's voyage to America when Divine Providence added the names of outsiders on the Mayflower's passenger list – forever entwining the destiny of those that history would refer to as "Strangers" and "Saints."

When the ship dropped anchor at Plymouth harbor in December of 1620, cold weather had set in, and the Pilgrims raced to build shelters on land. After a perilous journey across the Atlantic, many soon became ill due to a "powerful combination of scurvy, pneumonia, and tuberculosis… brought on by months of bad diet, cramped and unsanitary quarters, exposure and overexertion in all kinds of weather."[27] Sick passengers were cruelly kicked off the ship. Clean drinking water was scarce, and the only truly safe beverage to drink was in the ship's dwindling beer supply. The ship's crew selfishly hoarded this ale for themselves; those on land had little choice but to risk drinking contaminated water. When a sick passenger begged for even a tiny cup of ale to safely quench his thirst, one sailor callously replied: *"If you were my own father I wouldn't give you any!"*

But then disease even spread to the sailors, and "almost half of the crew died before they went away, and many of their officers and strongest men, amongst them the boatswain, gunner, three quartermasters, the cook and others."[28] The ship's once-healthy crew of hearty, robust sailors now languished in their sickbeds; cursing, complaining, and ruing the day they ever set foot on the ship. Friends who previously sang and drank together in jolly camaraderie now looked down on their infected shipmates with scorn, muttering: *"If they die, let them die!"* Seeing his crew in shambles, Captain Christopher Jones finally relented. He sent word to the Pilgrims on land and allowed them to rejoin the *Mayflower* for shelter and supplies.

After the Pilgrims reboarded the ship, they immediately began to help care for the ailing crew members. They showed the sailors "what pity they could, which made some of their hearts relent, such as the

ABOVE: To the right of *Law's* pedestal, the figure of *Mercy* stands with both hands faced open in humility, as if he is pleading for leniency.

boatswain [deck boss], who was an overbearing young man, and before would often curse and scoff at the passengers.

But when he grew weak, they [the Pilgrims] had compassion on him and helped him. Then he confessed he did not deserve it at their hands, for he had abused them in word and deed. *"'Oh,'* said he, *'I see now you show your love like Christians indeed to one another; but we let one another lie and die like dogs.'"[29]*

The Pilgrims displayed such mercy and compassion to the same men who had treated them so cruelly only days before, that it drew a deathbed conversion from one man in his final hours of life. For this contrite sailor, the mercy shown to him by the Pilgrims became a conduit for God's kindness, which "leads to repentance" (Romans 2:4).

These remarkable firsthand accounts were captured by William Bradford in his journals, which he kept to preserve the legacy of the Pilgrims at Plymouth Colony. Bradford's manuscripts were eventually published in the classic book, *Of Plimoth Plantation*, and have inspired generations since. Bradford's original journals were kept at Boston's Old South Church Library in Massachusetts until they vanished in the 1760s, reemerging nearly a century later in a London library. After years of negotiations, England returned Bradford's original manuscript to the Commonwealth of Massachusetts on May 26, 1897.

During the gift ceremony, Massachusetts Governor Roger Wolcott heralded the enduring legacy of the Pilgrims of Plymouth Colony, proclaiming: "Their feeble plantation became the birthplace of religious liberty, the cradle of a free Commonwealth. To them, a mighty nation owes its debt… May God in his mercy grant that the moral impulse which founded this nation may never cease to control its destiny."[30]

❶ PRAYER OF *Worship*

O Lord, you are my God; I will exalt you; I will praise your name, for you have done wonderful things, plans formed of old, faithful and sure. (Isaiah 25:1)

Worship God, the Ancient of Days, for the wonderful things He has done in your life.

❷ PRAYER OF *Confession*

Let us then approach God's throne of grace with confidence, so that we may receive mercy and find grace to help us in our time of need. (Hebrews 4:16)

I said, "Have mercy on me, Lord; heal me, for I have sinned against you." (Psalm 41:4)

Ask the Lord to forgive you of your sins, and thank Him for His great mercy.

❸ PRAYER OF *Petition*

Once you were not a people, but now you are God's people; once you had not received mercy, but now you have received mercy. Beloved, I urge you as sojourners and exiles to abstain from the passions of the flesh, which wage war against your soul. Keep your conduct among the Gentiles honorable, so that when they speak against you as evildoers, they may see your good deeds and glorify God on the day of visitation. (1 Peter 2:10-12)

Blessed be the God and Father of our Lord Jesus Christ, the Father of mercies and God of all comfort, who comforts us in all our affliction, so that we may be able to comfort those who are in any affliction, with the comfort with which we ourselves are comforted by God. (2 Corinthians 1:3-4)

Examine your own conduct as a believer. Does your behavior reveal the nature of Christ to others, or your own flesh? Ask the Holy Spirit to strengthen you in areas that you fall short. Recommit yourself to holiness. Consider the mercy and comfort God has shown you in your own seasons of trial and suffering. Ask the Holy Spirit to use these experiences to reveal God's grace and comfort to others.

4 PRANER OF *Intercession*

As for you, you were dead in your transgressions and sins, in which you used to live when you followed the ways of this world and of the ruler of the kingdom of the air, the spirit who is now at work in those who are disobedient. All of us also lived among them at one time, gratifying the cravings of our flesh and following its desires and thoughts. Like the rest, we were by nature deserving of wrath. But because of his great love for us, God, who is rich in mercy, made us alive with Christ even when we were dead in transgressions – it is by grace you have been saved. (Ephesians 2:1-5)

"I am sending you to them to open their eyes and turn them from darkness to light, and from the power of Satan to God, so that they may receive forgiveness of sins and a place among those who are sanctified by faith in me." (Acts 26:17-18)

Pray for those in your life who are where you once were; lost, and spiritually dead in their sins. Ask the Holy Spirit for opportunities to demonstrate His saving grace in your life to others, and for God to turn them from darkness to light. Intercede for all believers in the Lord's Church, that we would walk in love and mercy even as we proclaim biblical truth.

5 PRAYER OF *Thanksgiving*

Praise be to the God and Father of our Lord Jesus Christ! In his great mercy he has given us new birth into a living hope through the resurrection of Jesus Christ from the dead, and into an inheritance that can never perish, spoil or fade . (1 Peter 1:3-4)

Thank God for His mercy in your life, and for a living hope through Jesus Christ that will never fade.

I *love* the Lord,
for he *heard* my
voice; he heard my
cry for *mercy.*

(Psalm 116:1)

MERCY

At Plymouth Colony, the Pilgrims endeavored to provide equal justice under the law according to the biblical mandate to "hate evil, love good; [and] maintain justice in the courts" (Amos 5:15). In legal deliberations, the early colonists enforced due process and applied a biblical standard of using at least two or three witnesses to ascertain the truth. In 1638, this practice was highlighted when several men were arrested for the robbery and murder of a Nipmuc Indian man.

Arthur Peach, the group's ringleader, was a former soldier whom William Bradford described as "out of means and loth to work, and taking to idle ways and company."[31] After seducing a maidservant and running up several personal debts, Peach skipped town with friends and traveled from Massachusetts Bay into Narragansett country. Stopping to rest by the side of a footpath one afternoon, Peach and his friends looked up and recognized a Nipmuc Indian they had passed on the path a day earlier.

"At length there came a Narragansett Indian by, who had been trading at the Bay, and had some cloth and beads with him. They had met him the day before, and now he was returning. Peach called him to come and drink tobacco with them, and he came and sat down. He had told the others he would kill the Indian and take his goods. The others were afraid; but Peach said, *'Hang the rogue, he has killed many of us.'* So they let him do as he would, and when he saw his opportunity, he took his rapier and ran the man through the body once or twice, and took from him five fathoms of wampum and three coats of cloth; and then they went their way, leaving him for dead."[32]

This vicious attack would have gone unpunished, except that, incredibly, "the Indian managed to scramble up when they had gone, and made shift to get home."[33] Staggering to reach members of his tribe, the victim lived long enough to identify his attackers, setting them off in quick pursuit. When the Indians finally captured Peach and his accomplices, they demanded justice from the authorities, and the case was sent back to Plymouth for a trial. The jury delivered a guilty verdict, and the men were hanged. Justice was served that day, despite the objections of some colonists that William Bradford singled out for their ignorance.

"Nevertheless, some of the more ignorant colonists objected that

an Englishman should be put to death for an Indian. So at last the murderers were brought home… and after being tried and the evidence produced, they all in the end freely confessed to all the Indian had accused them of, and that they had done it in the manner described. So they were condemned by the jury, and executed.

ABOVE: To the left of *Law's* pedestal, the figure of *Justice* is shown with scales in one hand and a sword in the other.

"Some of the Narragansett Indians and the murdered man's friends were present when it was done, which gave them and all the country satisfaction. But it was a matter of much sadness to them here, as it was the second execution since they came— both being for willful murder."[34]

Bradford's narrative of the event is compelling. By describing certain colonists as "ignorant," he affirms the moral superiority of providing equal justice under the law. Similarly, by noting that "all the country" took satisfaction in the guilty verdict and ensuing punishment, Bradford proves that "When justice is done, it brings joy to the righteous but terror to evildoers." (Proverbs 21:15).

As believers, the Pilgrims understood their responsibility to enforce biblical justice to maintain freedom and liberty at Plymouth Colony. This requirement was articulated by British statesman Edmund Burke, who wrote: "What is liberty without wisdom and without virtue? It is the greatest of all possible evils; for it is folly, vice, and madness, without restraint. Men are qualified for civil liberty in exact proportion to their disposition to put moral chains upon their own appetites… Society cannot exist, unless a controlling power upon *will* and *appetite* be placed somewhere; and the less of it there is within, the more there must be without… men of intemperate minds cannot be free. Their passions forge their fetters [chains]."[35]

① PRAYER OF *Worship*

Righteousness and justice are the foundation of your throne; love and faithfulness go before you. (Psalm 89:14)

Praise Almighty God who rules from a throne of righteousness and justice.

② PRAYER OF *Confession*

He is the Rock, his works are perfect, and all his ways are just. A faithful God who does no wrong, upright and just is he. (Deuteronomy 32:4)

Confess your sins to a perfect and just God; thank the Lord for His mercy and forgiveness.

③ PRAYER OF *Petition*

Arise, Lord, in your anger; rise up against the rage of my enemies. Awake, my God; decree justice. (Psalm 7:6)

Then Jesus told his disciples a parable to show them that they should always pray and not give up. He said: "In a certain town there was a judge who neither feared God nor cared what people thought. And there was a widow in that town who kept coming to him with the plea, 'Grant me justice against my adversary.' For some time he refused. But finally he said to himself, 'Even though I don't fear God or care what people think, yet because this widow keeps bothering me, I will see that she gets justice, so that she won't eventually come and attack me!'" And the Lord said, "Listen to what the unjust judge says. And will not God bring about justice for his chosen ones, who cry out to him day and night? Will he keep putting them off? I tell you, he will see that they get justice, and quickly. However, when the Son of Man comes, will he find faith on the earth?" (Luke 18:1-8)

If you carry a burden of an injustice in some area of your life, bring your heart before the Lord. Ask God to bind up your wounds, and heal you of any anger or bitterness. Pray for those who have wounded you. If you harbor any resentment toward God over your circumstances, repent. Faithfully plead your case before Him, and ask for divine vindication. Ask God to "fill your mouth with laughter and your lips with shouts of joy" as you wait on Him. (Job 8:21)

❹ PRAYER OF *Intercession*

Learn to do right; seek justice. Defend the oppressed. Take up the cause of the fatherless; plead the case of the widow. (Isaiah 1:17)

For Christ also suffered once for sins, the righteous for the unrighteous, to bring you to God. He was put to death in the body but made alive in the Spirit. (1 Peter 3:18)

The Lord works righteousness and justice for all the oppressed. (Psalm 103:6)

I know that the Lord secures justice for the poor and upholds the cause of the needy. (Psalm 140:12)

But let justice roll on like a river, righteousness like a never-failing stream! (Amos 5:24)

William Bradford heralded justice over ignorance in the case of Arthur Peach. Pray for our nation today, which is deeply polarized over issues of inequality and injustice. Lift up any specific areas of injustice that the Lord has put on your heart; ask the Holy Spirit to reveal how you can contribute toward a solution. Bind the spirit of division that is attacking America. Pray for a spirit of reconciliation and unity to arise in our nation, bringing repentance, forgiveness, and healing. Intercede for our judges and court systems, that God would use them to deliver justice to all in our nation. Pray for the Lord's Church, that we would be God's instrument on earth to defend the oppressed and seek justice for the weak and marginalized.

❺ PRAYER OF *Thanksgiving*

Of the greatness of his government and peace there will be no end. He will reign on David's throne and over his kingdom, establishing and upholding it with justice and righteousness from that time on and forever. The zeal of the Lord Almighty will accomplish this. (Isaiah 9:7)

Give thanks for eternal reign of the Lord Jesus Christ, of which there will be no end.

"Your *throne,* O God, will last for ever and *ever;* a *scepter* of justice will be the scepter of your *kingdom.*"

(Hebrews 1:8)

WISDOME AND GIVES BEING
TO ALL VERSES. THAT ARE
AND AS ONE SMALL CANDLE
MAY LIGHT A THOUSAND SO
THE LIGHT HERE KINDLED
HATH SPRED INTO MANY. YEA
IN SOME SORT TO OUR WHOLE
NATION. YET THE GLORIE
IS NOT OF MAN CAN HAVE ALL
THE PRAISE.

GOVERNOR WILLIAM BRADFORD

64

EDUCATION

Education

DAY 8

Most of the Pilgrims came from humble backgrounds as merchants or laborers, and only a select few had the benefit of a university education. As the spiritual leaders of the church, Pastor John Robinson and Elder William Brewster each "brought the tradition of learning from Cambridge and influenced the people of Plymouth, who looked up to them as their intellectual and spiritual guides."[36]

As a congregation, the Pilgrims were inquisitive and eager for knowledge; they were known to spend hours in church discussing the deepest theological concepts of their day. "Pinning their faith on the scriptures and on reason, the Pilgrims dared to grapple with the profundities of faith and controversial concepts like the sovereignty of God, predestination, salvation, eschatology, biblical exegesis, the nature of the church, and the limits of civil authority."[37]

There were no formal schools in the early years of Plymouth Colony, and children were educated at home – their own or that of a neighboring family. The family unit acted as a school, and each child's education began "at the mother's knee, and often ended in the cornfield or barn by the father's side."[38] As parents, the Pilgrims believed it was their God-given responsibility to teach children how to be faithful Christians and productive members of society, and that if you "train up a child in the way he should go; even when he is old he will not depart from it" (Proverbs 22:6).

Even the youngest children participated in daily family devotions, where the Bible was "read and recited, quoted and consulted… committed to memory and constantly searched for meaning" in the home.[39] Relying on the rich stories and moral lessons in Scripture, the process of instilling morals, literacy, and manners into children was seamlessly incorporated into the daily routines of life. Although both parents played a significant role in each child's training and development, women were the primary educators in the home.

Armed with love and discipline, "colonial mothers often achieved more than our modern-day elementary schools with their federally funded programs and education specialists. These colonial mothers used simple, time-tested methods of instruction mixed with plain, old-fashioned hard work."[40]

For the Pilgrims, the greatest aim of literacy was to equip their children to understand and interpret Scripture for themselves. Using the Geneva Bible and a book of worship called the Ainsworth Psalter, the goal of all Pilgrim parents was to "instruct their children in the principles of religion, good manners, and civil behavior; to inculcate in them reverence for their elders and superiors; to bring them up in some lawful and gainful calling; to teach them to read and write for both worldly and spiritual ends."[41]

Relying on the Bible and using practical, hands-on instruction, the Pilgrims educated their children in a manner that may seem primitive compared to our modern systems of public education. "Yet for two hundred years in American history, from the mid-1600s to the mid-1800s, public schools as we know them today were virtually non-existent, and… the educational needs of America were met by the free market. In these two centuries, America produced several generations of highly skilled and literate men and women who laid the foundation for a nation dedicated to the principles of freedom and self-government."[42]

With the arrival of the Geneva Bible at Plymouth Colony, the influence of Scripture in teaching literacy became embedded in America's educational roots. Seventy years after the Pilgrims landed at Plymouth, children across New England were learning to read using the nation's first textbook: *The New-England Primer.* Featuring the Ten Commandments, the Golden Rule, a catechism, poetry, and prose, this book became a formative tool of learning in early American households, second only to the Bible itself. It shaped the young lives of many future leaders, such as John Adams, Benjamin Franklin, and John Hancock, and "our founding fathers were weaned on these beliefs."[43]

"The only *foundation* for a useful education in a *republic* is to be laid in religion. Without this, there can be no *virtue,* and without virtue there can be no *liberty,* and liberty is the object and *life* of all republican governments."

- Benjamin Rush (1745-1813), physician, abolitionist, educator, politician, and signer of the Declaration of Independence

① PRAYER OF *Worship*

Who has measured the waters in the hollow of his hand, or with the breadth of his hand marked off the heavens? Who has held the dust of the earth in a basket, or weighed the mountains on the scales and the hills in a balance? Who can fathom the Spirit of the Lord, or instruct the Lord as his counselor? Whom did the Lord consult to enlighten him, and who taught him the right way? Who was it that taught him knowledge, or showed him the path of understanding? (Isaiah 40:12-14)

Great is the Lord and most worthy of praise; his greatness no one can fathom. One generation commends your works to another; they tell of your mighty acts... I will meditate on your wonderful works. (Psalm 145:3-5)

Pause and meditate on the glorious splendor of God's majesty, and praise Him for His mighty acts as the Creator of all heaven and earth.

② PRAYER OF *Confession*

Lord, I wait for you; you will answer, Lord my God. I confess my iniquity; I am troubled by my sin. Come quickly to help me, my Lord and my Savior. (Psalm 38:15, 18, 22)

Heal me, Lord, and I will be healed; save me and I will be saved, for you are the one I praise. (Jeremiah 17:14)

Spend a moment to wait before God. If you are struggling with any sins, hurts, or lingering offenses — pour your heart out to Him. Repent for your sins, and ask God to heal you. Praise Him for forgiveness and restoration.

③ PRAYER OF *Petition*

I remind you to fan into flame the gift of God... for the Spirit God gave us does not make us timid, but gives us power, love and self-discipline. What you heard from me, keep as the pattern of sound teaching, with faith and love in Christ Jesus. (2 Timothy 1:6-7, 13)

I pray that you, being rooted and established in love, may have power, together with all the Lord's holy people, to grasp how wide and long and high and deep is the love of Christ, and to know this love that surpasses knowledge–that you may be filled to the measure of all the fullness of God. (Ephesians 3:17-19)

But as for you, continue in what you have learned and have become convinced of, because you know those from whom you learned it, and how from infancy you have known the Holy Scriptures, which are able to make you wise for salvation through faith in Christ Jesus. All Scripture is God-breathed and is useful for teaching... so that the servant of God may be thoroughly equipped for every good work. (2 Timothy 3:1-5, 14-17)

Always be prepared to give an answer to everyone who asks you to give the reason for the hope that you have. (1 Peter 3:15)

His divine power has given us everything we need for a godly life through our knowledge of him who called us by his own glory and goodness. For this very reason, make every effort to add to your faith goodness; and to goodness, knowledge; and to knowledge, self-control; and to self-control, perseverance; and to perseverance, godliness; and to godliness, mutual affection; and to mutual affection, love. For if you possess these qualities in increasing measure, they will keep you from being ineffective and unproductive in your knowledge of our Lord Jesus Christ. (2 Peter 1:3, 5-8)

Even while living in Holland's secular, immoral culture — the Pilgrims were diligent to instill biblical faith and virtue in their children. If you are parenting in today's increasingly secular environment, ask God for the strength to lead your family in God's truth. Pray for the courage to model a godly example to your children in a world that is hostile to people of faith. Talk openly with them about the challenges of living out their faith in a world of "cancel culture." Find practical tools to help them understand and defend their faith. Ask the Holy Spirit to reveal the unique gifts and talents within each of your children; cultivate them. If you feel like you've failed your children in the past, don't give up! Start fresh today and ask God for divine strategies to redeem the time and make an impact on your family. Pray for boldness to live a godly life in these last days. Ask the Holy Spirit to help you be disciplined in studying God's word, so you can effectively share the reason for your hope in Christ and be thoroughly equipped for every good work.

④ PRAYER OF *Intercession*

The lips of the wise spread knowledge, but the hearts of fools are not upright. Those who disregard discipline despise themselves, but the one who heeds correction gains understanding. Wisdom's instruction is to fear the Lord, and humility comes before honor. (Proverbs 15:7, 32-33)

Get wisdom, get understanding; do not forget my words or turn away from them. Hold on to instruction, do not let it go; guard it well, for it is your life. (Proverbs 4:5, 13)

Pray for our nation's educators; for the teachers, parents, family members, and mentors who train and influence children. Ask God to bring the light of truth to our educational system, and raise up bold leaders who will fight to restore sound instruction in our schools. Pray for the Lord to visit our college and university campuses, and spark a revival of truth that leads to salvation. Pray for the rapid rise of homeschooling and educational cooperatives across the nation; ask God to raise up leaders in this movement, and strengthen those who are stepping out in faith to educate their children. Ask the Holy Spirit to train and transform our children and young adults in virtue, knowledge, and biblical truth.

⑤ PRAYER OF *Thanksgiving*

Know therefore that the Lord your God is God; he is the faithful God, keeping his covenant of love to a thousand generations of those who love him and keep his commandments. (Deuteronomy 7:9)

Out of his fullness we have all received grace in place of grace already given. For the law was given through Moses; grace and truth came through Jesus Christ. (John 1:16-17)

I have loved you with an everlasting love; I have drawn you with unfailing kindness. (Jeremiah 31:3)

Consider the unfathomable faithfulness of Almighty God, who keeps His covenant of love to a thousand generations. Thank the Lord for His everlasting love, and for the grace and truth we received through Jesus Christ, His Son.

EDUCATION

EDUCATION

WISDOM

Wisdom

As a church congregation, the Pilgrims were guided by men of great character, humility, and moral conviction. These rare leadership qualities were fully matched among their female counterparts: the brave Pilgrim women who displayed an equal measure of faith and courage under pressure. Although the colonists undoubtedly made mistakes, they were sincere people of faith who believed: "If any of you lacks wisdom, you should ask God, who gives generously to all without finding fault, and it will be given to you" (James 1:5). Through the wisdom of leaders such as John Robinson, John Carver, William Brewster, and William Bradford, the colonists were able to moderate conflict, persevere in the face of sickness and death, and, in time, even achieve prosperity in Plymouth Colony.

Although he died before joining his beloved church at Plymouth Colony, no one wielded more influence over the Pilgrims than their pastor, John Robinson. Robinson was a towering example to his congregation, professing his ardent "desire to learn further, or better, what the good will of God is… and faithfully… embrace and walk in the truth."[44] Like a good father readying his children for a difficult journey, he worked tirelessly to prepare his church for the daunting task of building a new colony in America. The voyage alone was dangerous. Even if his members safely reached land, Robinson knew it would only be the first of many trials that would test them.

To prepare them, Pastor Robinson cautioned his members against "the deadly plague of comfort," and urged them to maintain the bonds of unity.[45] When outsiders joined their venture, Robinson urged them to be considerate of those outside their faith, and "watchful that we ourselves neither give, nor easily take, offense."[46] Robinson's influence is evident throughout the words of the Mayflower Compact, and his words of faith, prudence, and wisdom were a guiding force for the Pilgrims at Plymouth Colony.

When Robinson chose to stay behind and tend to the remaining members of the congregation in Holland, he appointed Elder William Brewster as spiritual leader of the Pilgrims sailing to America. Brewster delivered two sermons faithfully every Sunday at Plymouth Colony for years before a formal minister arrived to replace him. Affable and kind, he was deeply loved by the congregation. When Brewster passed away at 77, his death was a great loss to everyone in the colony – especially William Bradford.

ABOVE: To the right of *Education's* pedestal, *Wisdom* is shown looking up for divine insight as he stands near tools of learning such books, an atlas, and the Ten Commandments.

Bradford had lost his own father as a young boy and was only 14 when he joined the church in Scrooby, England. Young William spent countless hours with Brewster studying the Bible, Latin, and Greek, and their relationship was like a father and son. Bradford eulogized Brewster as being "wise and discreet and well spoken… of a very cheerful spirit… inoffensive and innocent in his life and conversation," and loved by all who knew him.[47] Hand-picked by Pastor Robinson for his mature faith and leadership, Brewster led the church through countless trials, and his life "was a product of the Pilgrim ethics."[48]

When it came time to elect leaders, John Carver was an obvious choice to serve as Plymouth's first governor. As a trusted deacon and leader in the church, Carver's wisdom and diplomacy with Chief Massasoit fostered a peace treaty with the Wampanoags that endured for over 50 years. When Carver died unexpectedly in 1621, 31-year-old Bradford was elected to replace him. Though Bradford was reluctant to assume the role of governor, once in office, he proved "talented and indefatigable, [and] passionately devoted to the welfare of New Plimoth."[49] Bradford would become Plymouth's longest-serving governor, and he exemplified the Pilgrim way of life.

As an astute observer of the Bible and human nature, Bradford "worked well with men because he loved and honored them as God's creatures, the end and purpose of the divine scheme."[50] Although he never attended college, Bradford was a curious, self-taught scholar who spent decades gleaning wisdom from Robinson and Brewster. At Plymouth Colony, Governor Bradford kept a library of over 400 books for personal study and teaching. In his later years, he devoted himself to learning Hebrew because he longed "to see with mine own eyes, something of that most ancient language… in which the law and oracles of God were [written]… from the creation."[51] Characterized as "a genuine Christian and a consummate politician," Bradford was Plymouth's most enduring leader in church and government.[52]

1 PRAYER OF *Worship*

Stand up and praise the Lord your God, who is from everlasting to everlasting. Blessed be your glorious name, and may it be exalted above all blessing and praise. You alone are the Lord. You made the heavens, even the highest heavens, and all their starry host, the earth and all that is on it, the seas and all that is in them. You give life to everything, and the multitudes of heaven worship you. (Nehemiah 9:5-6)

In your own words, praise the glorious name of the Lord your God, who is from everlasting to everlasting.

2 PRAYER OF *Confession*

Whoever conceals their sins does not prosper, but the one who confesses and renounces them finds mercy. (Proverbs 28:13)

Confess your sins to a merciful God, and thank Him for forgiveness.

3 PRAYER OF *Petition*

But the wisdom that comes from heaven is first of all pure; then peace-loving, considerate, submissive, full of mercy and good fruit, impartial and sincere. (James 3:17)

Be very careful, then, how you live—not as unwise but as wise, making the most of every opportunity, because the days are evil. (Ephesians 5:15-16)

Be wise in the way you act toward outsiders; make the most of every opportunity. Let your conversation be always full of grace, seasoned with salt, so that you may know how to answer everyone. (Colossians 4:5-6)

Consider areas in your life where you need wisdom and guidance, and ask the Holy Spirit for direction and discernment. Meditate on Proverbs and other books of wisdom in the Bible. Ask God to help you cultivate a heart of wisdom that makes the most of every divine opportunity and bears much fruit.

④ PRAYER OF *Intercession*

When the righteous thrive, the people rejoice; when the wicked rule, the people groan. (Proverbs 29:2)

In the Lord's hand the king's heart is a stream of water that he channels toward all who please him. (Proverbs 21:1)

Fools give full vent to their rage, but the wise bring calm in the end. (Proverbs 29:11)

For lack of guidance a nation falls, but victory is won through many advisers. (Proverbs 11:14)

Follow my example, as I follow the example of Christ. (1 Corinthians 11:1)

Do not be wise in your own eyes; fear the Lord and shun evil. (Proverbs 3:7)

The Pilgrims valued wisdom, and they followed leaders who led by example according to God's word. Pray for the leaders in your life; ask the Lord to give them divine wisdom to lead and influence others for the glory of God. Pray for God's leaders and servants in the global Church; ask the Lord to give them wise strategies for every obstacle or challenge. Pray for America; ask God to raise up leaders across the nation who will seek God for wisdom in this hour. Pray for the leaders of all nations; ask God to cause their hearts — their thoughts, words, and decisions — to align with His eternal purposes.

⑤ PRAYER OF *Thanksgiving*

My shield is God Most High, who saves the upright in heart. I will give thanks to the Lord because of his righteousness; I will sing the praises of the name of the Lord Most High. (Psalm 7:10,17)

Give thanks to God Most High, our strength and shield, who saves the upright in heart through the sacrifice of His Son, Jesus.

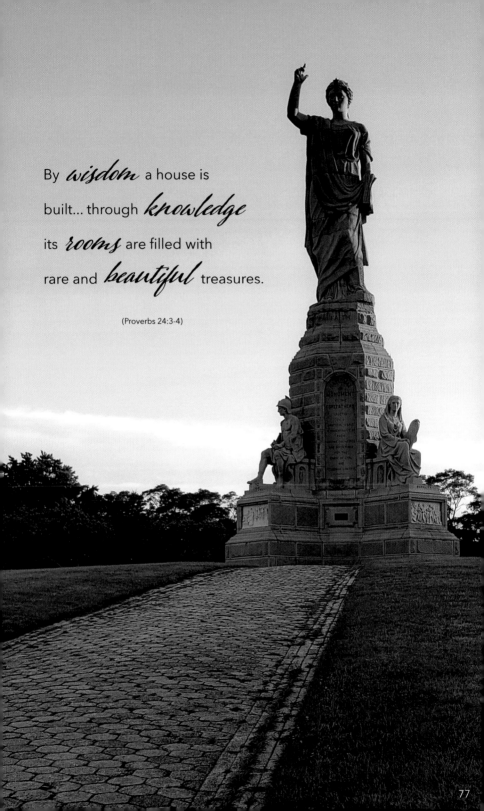

By *wisdom* a house is built... through *knowledge* its *rooms* are filled with rare and *beautiful* treasures.

(Proverbs 24:3-4)

After building a new life at Plymouth Colony, the Pilgrims looked back on the years they spent in Holland and recalled: "How hard the country was where we lived, how many spent their estate in it… how unable we were to give such good education to our children as we received."[53] Although Holland allowed the Pilgrims to worship God freely, it also exacted a steep price in other areas. In Leiden, entire families worked long hours outside of the home to make ends meet.

William Bradford spoke of the burden this placed on their children, writing that "necessity was a task-master over them… their dearest children; which not a little wounded the hearts of many a loving father and mother, and produced many sad and sorrowful effects. Many of their children, who were of the best disposition… [and] willing to bear part of their parents' burden, were often so oppressed with their labours, that though their minds were free and willing, their bodies bowed under the weight."[54]

Such a draining lifestyle of constant work deprived Pilgrim families of quality time together, making it difficult for parents to impart faith and values to their children. Many of their children became discouraged by the relentless cycle of work. Others became enticed by "the many temptations of the city… [and] were led by evil example into dangerous courses… leaving their parents. Some became soldiers, others embarked upon voyages by sea and others upon worse courses tending to dissoluteness and the danger of their souls, to the great grief of the parents and the dishonour of God."[55]

As the years passed by in Holland, the Pilgrims watched as their legacy began slipping away. They hoped America would offer better opportunities to educate and influence their children – and it did. In their new settlement at Plymouth Colony, "young and old were together most of the time. The family was the center for teaching morality… and building Christian character. Youth were admonished and guided, and the unruly were disciplined… and a sustaining faith was created and rooted in the spiritual values of the Bible."[56]

The Pilgrims understood the importance of God's design for the family unit to forge and preserve future generations. At Plymouth Colony, "the colonists were sustained by a family comradeship. There was a Bible in almost every home… which established standards

ABOVE: To the left of *Education's* pedestal, *Youth* is depicted by a mother and her child. To symbolize relationship as teacher and student, the mother holds a book and the child holds a paper scroll.

of conduct and faith... under which men and women faced the testings of birth, sickness, death, housework, farm labor, hunger, sorrow, and joy."[57]

During their first winter at Plymouth Colony, the Pilgrims encountered a brutal epidemic that wiped out entire families. Of the 18 wives who crossed the Atlantic on the *Mayflower,* only four survived. Women sacrificed themselves to care for sick children, and because of this, young boys and girls had a much higher survival rate.

The few mothers who lived took newly orphaned children into their homes to be raised as their own. Although the colony was decimated by sickness that first year, "the fifty-one survivors were able to endure in large measure because they were part of firmly knit households."[58]

William and Alice Bradford were powerful examples of how God used surrogate families to protect and preserve young lives in the new settlement for His divine purposes. "Bradford was taking care of Robert Cushman's son, Thomas, when the father died on a colony mission in London. He later adopted the lad... [and] the Bradfords also raised Nathaniel Morton. These two youths developed into foremost leaders of the colony."[59]

➊ PRAYER OF *Worship*

Who can fathom the Spirit of the Lord, or instruct the Lord as his counselor? The Lord is the everlasting God, the Creator of the ends of the earth. He will not grow tired or weary, and his understanding no one can fathom. He gives strength to the weary and increases the power of the weak. Even youths grow tired and weary, and young men stumble and fall; but those who hope in the Lord will renew their strength. They will soar on wings like eagles; they will run and not grow weary, they will walk and not be faint. (Isaiah 40:13, 28-31)

Offer praise and worship to the everlasting God, Creator of the ends of the earth.

➋ PRAYER OF *Confession*

This is what the Sovereign Lord, the Holy One of Israel, says: "In repentance and rest is your salvation, in quietness and trust is your strength." (Isaiah 30:15)

Come before the Sovereign Lord with a heart of repentance, and be strengthened.

➌ PRAYER OF *Petition*

These commandments that I give you today are to be on your hearts. Impress them on your children. Talk about them when you sit at home and when you walk along the road, when you lie down and when you get up. (Deuteronomy 6:6-7)

Jesus replied: "Love the Lord your God with all your heart and with all your soul and with all your mind." (Matthew 22:37)

He is the Lord our God... He remembers his covenant forever, the promise he made, for a thousand generations. (Psalm 105:7-8)

Pray for your children, or any youth God has placed in your life. Ask the Lord to guard their hearts from evil, and to reveal Himself to them in a personal way. Pray for opportunities to spend quality time together. Ask the Holy Spirit for influence over their young hearts, and teach them about God. Dedicate your children to the Lord, who is faithful to a thousand generations.

➍ PRAYER OF *Intercession*

Don't let anyone look down on you because you are young, but set an example for the believers in speech, in conduct, in love, in faith and in purity. (1 Timothy 4:12)

The Lord then said to Noah, "Go into the ark, you and your whole family, because I have found you righteous in this generation." (Genesis 7:1)

Flee the evil desires of youth and pursue righteousness, faith, love and peace, along with those who call on the Lord out of a pure heart. (2 Timothy 2:22)

For the eyes of the Lord range throughout the earth to strengthen those whose hearts are fully committed to him. (2 Chronicles 16:9)

Pray for our nation's children and young adults, who are confronted by evil in this nation on a daily basis. Ask God to strengthen the hearts of those who are living for Him, and to give them influence over their peers. Pray for the Holy Spirit to ignite revival among our youth — and send the hope of Christ to a generation that is angry, addicted, cynical, and weary. Ask God to raise up a righteous remnant of youth who will call on the Lord with a pure heart. Pray for God to raise up mature believers in the Body of Christ who will sacrifice of themselves to serve young people as friends, mentors, and teachers — breaking generational curses and leaving a legacy of faith.

➎ PRAYER OF *Thanksgiving*

Because of the Lord's great love we are not consumed, for his compassions never fail. They are new every morning; great is your faithfulness. (Lamentations 3:22-23)

Thank God for his unfailing love and faithfulness in your life.

From the *rising* of the sun to the *place* where it sets, the *name* of the Lord is to be *praised.*

(Psalm 113:3)

LIBERTY

84

The Pilgrims established many new freedoms at Plymouth Colony, but the first of these – and the underlying theme of their entire story – was religious liberty. The Pilgrims risked their lives crossing the Atlantic to find a place where they could freely worship and share the gospel, and they found it in America. Unlike the religious tyranny they suffered in England, at Plymouth Colony the Pilgrims could practice their faith without fear of retribution. "No one in America would be raiding their Sunday services to stop their worship. Neither would they be hauled off to jail because of their beliefs, nor ever again forced to flee their homes because of their faith. And the way of freedom they had blazed in the wilds of the New World would eventually become the path of liberty for countless people from around the world; people yearning for a new life, a new start, a new home – and who would find it as Americans."[60]

In time, Plymouth Colony also achieved economic freedom. After striking a deal with London investors to finance their trip to America, the Pilgrims agreed to share the colony's profits until their debt was paid. "On arrival in Plymouth the settlers faced the superhuman task of building homes, planting crops, and starting debt payments."[61] For the first three years, the settlement operated as a communal economy while the colonists worked to fulfill the terms of their contract. However, communal farming inevitably led to inequality – some colonists labored hard, and others less. Regardless of individual effort, the outcome was the same. It wasn't long before many became resentful.

According to William Bradford: "The young men who were most able and fit for service objected to being forced to spend their time and strength in working for other men's wives and children, without any recompense. The strong man or the resourceful man had no more share of food, clothes, etc., than the weak man who was not able to do a quarter the other could. This was thought injustice. As for men's wives who were obliged to do service for other men… many husbands would not brook it."[62]

Bradford said further: "Let none argue that this is due to human failing, rather than to this communistic plan of life in itself. I answer, seeing that all men have this failing in them, that God in His wisdom saw that another plan of life was fitter for them."[63] Bradford ordered a return to private enterprise.

"The governor, with the advice of the chief among them, allowed each man to plant corn for his own household, and to trust to themselves for that. Every family was assigned a parcel of land, according to the proportion of their number... This was very successful. It made all hands very industrious, so that much more corn was planted than otherwise would have been."[64] In their first year at Plymouth, the Pilgrims reaped a meager harvest from 26 acres of shared land, and they struggled to survive. In their second year, the colony increased its production to 60 acres. In their third year, after switching to private enterprise, the colonists planted an astounding 184 acres. Under this capitalistic model, the Pilgrims thrived, and the community "shaped itself to become, unknowingly, the pattern for a great democracy."[65]

The Pilgrims also achieved constitutional liberty. Building on the Mayflower Compact, in 1636, they produced the Pilgrim Code of Law, which secured the rights of all citizens in the first basic constitution of the New World. The Pilgrim Code of Law outlined the government's role, not to *grant* liberty of itself, but rather to *protect* those liberties inherently granted *by God*. The Pilgrims recognized that liberty came from God, not from the state— a belief that became embedded in America's DNA. "The treasured liberties championed by America's Founding Fathers were in huge measure part of their heritage from the *Mayflower* Pilgrims. Their biblically based values and principles would become the foundation of the United States of America."[66]

In 1776, our Founders enshrined these undeniable truths on America's birth certificate: "We hold these truths to be self-evident, that all men are created equal, that they are endowed by their Creator with certain unalienable Rights, that among these are Life, Liberty and the pursuit of Happiness. That to secure these rights, Governments are instituted among Men, deriving their just powers from the consent of the governed."[67] The Pilgrim seeds of liberty had taken firm hold, bearing extraordinary fruit.

From the raging waves that first pushed the *Mayflower* north into the safety of Plymouth Harbor, to the men who signed their "support of this Declaration, with a firm reliance on the protection of Divine Providence… [pledging] to each other our lives, our fortunes, and our sacred honor," a nation was formed by the providence of Almighty God.[68] As a result, Samuel Adams observed: "We have this day, restored the Sovereign to whom alone men ought to be obedient. He reigns in heaven… from the rising to the setting sun, may His kingdom come."[69]

Where the Spirit
of the *Lord* is,
there is *freedom.*

(2 Corinthians 3:17)

87

❶ PRAYER OF *Worship*

You, God, are my God, earnestly I seek you; I thirst for you, my whole being longs for you, in a dry and parched land where there is no water. I have seen you in the sanctuary and beheld your power and your glory. Because your love is better than life, my lips will glorify you. I will praise you as long as I live, and in your name I will lift up my hands. (Psalm 63:1-4)

Praise the Lord, my soul, and forget not all his benefits—who forgives all your sins and heals all your diseases, who redeems your life from the pit and crowns you with love and compassion, who satisfies your desires with good things so that your youth is renewed like the eagle's. (Psalm 103:2-5)

Pause and reflect on your eternal inheritance as a child of God. In your own words, glorify God and worship Him with your own lips.

❷ PRAYER OF *Confession*

For the sake of your name, Lord, forgive my iniquity, though it is great. (Psalm 25:11)

Who is a God like you, who pardons sin and forgives the transgression of the remnant of his inheritance? You do not stay angry forever but delight to show mercy. (Micah 7:18)

Acknowledge your sins before God, and praise Him for His enduring mercy.

❸ PRAYER OF *Petition*

Do not merely listen to the word, and so deceive yourselves. Do what it says. (James 1:22)

It is for freedom that Christ has set us free. Stand firm, then, and do not let yourselves be burdened again by a yoke of slavery. You, my brothers and sisters, were called to be free. But do not use your freedom to indulge the flesh; rather, serve one another humbly in love. For the entire law is fulfilled in keeping this one command: "Love your neighbor as yourself." (Galatians 5:1,13-14)

So if the Son sets you free, you will be free indeed. (John 8:36)

Our conscience testifies that we have conducted ourselves in the world, and especially in our relations with you, with integrity and godly sincerity. We have done so, relying not on worldly wisdom but on God's grace. (2 Corinthians 1:12)

Let us hold unswervingly to the hope we profess, for he who promised is faithful. And let us consider how we may spur one another on toward love and good deeds, not giving up meeting together, as some are in the habit of doing, but encouraging one another—and all the more as you see the Day approaching. (Hebrews 10:23-25)

From the very start of their voyage to America, God called the Pilgrims to live and work alongside those who did not share their beliefs. As a result, many converted to Christianity after seeing their sincere demonstration of faith. Reflect on your own walk with the Lord. As you consider how Christ has set you free from sin, pray that you would not use your freedom to indulge the flesh, but to serve others in love. Ask the Holy Spirit to empower you with a bold witness and godly sincerity — so others will encounter Christ through your example of faith.

4 PRAYER OF *Intercession*

The Spirit of the Sovereign Lord is on me, because the Lord has anointed me to proclaim good news to the poor. He has sent me to bind up the brokenhearted, to proclaim freedom for the captives and release from darkness for the prisoners. (Isaiah 61:1)

Now the Lord is the Spirit, and where the Spirit of the Lord is, there is freedom. And we all, who with unveiled faces contemplate the Lord's glory, are being transformed into his image with ever-increasing glory, which comes from the Lord, who is the Spirit. (2 Corinthians 3:17-18)

If my people, who are called by my name, will humble themselves and pray and seek my face and turn from their wicked ways, then I will hear from heaven, and I will forgive their sin and will heal their land. (1 Chronicles 7:14)

Or do you show contempt for the riches of his kindness, forbearance and patience, not realizing that God's kindness is intended to lead you to repentance? (Romans 2:4)

Restore us again, God our Savior, and put away your displeasure toward us. Will you not revive us again, that your people may rejoice in you? Show us your unfailing love, Lord, and grant us your salvation. (Psalm 85:4, 6-7)

The Pilgrims sailed to America over 400 years ago to advance the gospel and today, our country holds the largest Christian population in the world — and America is synonymous with liberty. But there is no freedom without the Spirit of the Lord, and over the years America's God-given liberties have slowly eroded in the chaos of godless pursuits and secularism. Pray for America. In God's unfailing love, ask the Lord to heal our land and to revive our nation's biblical foundations. Pray for a civic reawakening of all Americans, and the knowledge that liberty comes from God, not the state. Pray for a spiritual revival of faith and freedom in America, that in God's mercy we would continue to spread the gospel to the nations as a model for civic and religious freedom.

⑤ PRAYER OF

By his power God raised the Lord from the dead, and he will raise us also. (1 Corinthians 6:14)

The Lord is my rock, my fortress and my deliverer; my God is my rock, in whom I take refuge, my shield and the horn of my salvation. He is my stronghold, my refuge and my savior. I called to the Lord, who is worthy of praise, and have been saved from my enemies. You, Lord, are my lamp; the Lord turns my darkness into light. With your help I can advance against a troop; with my God I can scale a wall. As for God, his way is perfect: The Lord's word is flawless; he shields all who take refuge in him. For who is God besides the Lord? And who is the Rock except our God? It is God who arms me with strength and keeps my way secure. (2 Samuel 22:2-3, 29-33)

Offer prayers of thanks to Almighty God, your strength and deliverer, who shields all who take refuge in Him.

PEACE

After landing in Plymouth, the Pilgrims sought to establish peace with the native population. Aided by the help of English-speaking Squanto as their translator, the Pilgrims were able to arrange an important meeting with Chief Massasoit, the grand sachem of the Wampanoag Indian tribe. When Chief Massasoit arrived at Plymouth Colony, Governor John Carver greeted him with great ceremony and respect, and showered him with gifts and entertainment. This diplomatic encounter resulted in the *Pilgrim-Wampanoag Peace Treaty,* a remarkable alliance that lasted over 50 years, fulfilling the Pilgrim's desire to "live at peace with everyone" (Romans 12:18).

As Christians, the Pilgrims didn't view peace as the *absence* of struggle in their lives; true peace was God's sustaining presence in the midst of it. During the early years of Plymouth Colony, the Pilgrims encountered extreme conditions of sickness, death, and lack. None of these circumstances made them doubt God was with them, and none of this caused anyone to turn back. In the Spring of 1621, Captain Christopher Jones steered the *Mayflower* out of Plymouth harbor to begin her return voyage home. Despite his astonishing offer of free passage to anyone who wished to leave, not a single Pilgrim was onboard.

William Bradford would reflect later on how God sustained them through their trials, writing: "by the good providence and blessing of God, we have enjoyed such plenty as though the windows of heaven had been opened to us. How few, weak, and raw were we at our first beginning… yet God wrought our peace for us."[70]

The Pilgrims viewed suffering as the inevitable mark of a well-lived Christian life. When Elder William Brewster died in 1644, William Bradford eulogized a close friend who had devoted his life to God and the Pilgrim congregation. "About the 18th of April died their reverend elder, my dear and loving friend, Mr. William Brewster, a man who had done and suffered much for the Lord Jesus and the gospel's sake, and had borne his part in weal or woe with this poor persecuted church for over thirty-five years in England, Holland, and this wilderness, and had done the Lord and them faithful service in his calling."[71] Continuing, Bradford wrote: "I would ask, was he the worse for any of his former sufferings? Nay; he was surely the better, for now they were added to his honour."[72]

ABOVE: To the right of *Liberty's* pedestal, the figure of *Peace* holds an olive branch, and stands with a cornucopia at her feet.

Throughout many trials, the Pilgrims demonstrated a peace that is not of this world. They were encouraged by the words of their pastor, John Robinson, who articulated the reward for all who place their trust in Jesus: "Great shall be his security and peace in all dangers, sweet his comfort in all distresses, with happy deliverance from all evil, whether in life or in death."[73] In their deepest valley of suffering, the Pilgrims were sustained by an abiding peace that pointed others to the source of their strength: Jesus Christ.

"The question... has been asked before, how it happened, that a company of wanderers, without military force and with little wealth... could endure such trials... and this question finds its answer in the religious character of the Colony. Worldly objects were with them secondary, and political ambition found no place among them. Religious faith enabled them to do and endure, under a sense of duty, and for the sake of God and humanity, what no mere selfish purpose was ever yet able to accomplish. They were men [and women] that feared God, and could lay down their lives for a principle; and so they lived and 'died in faith, not having received the promises, but having seen them afar off, and were persuaded of them, and embraced them, and confessed that they were strangers and pilgrims on the earth.'"[74]

As followers of Christ, the Pilgrims identified with the words of the Apostle Paul, who wrote: "I consider my life worth nothing to me; my only aim is to finish the race and complete the task the Lord Jesus has given me – the task of testifying to the good news of God's grace" (Acts 20:24). Throughout their story, the Pilgrims devoted their lives to God's glorious purposes. Christ alone was their peace.

❶ PRAYER OF *Worship*

I lift up my eyes to the mountains— where does my help come from? My help comes from the Lord, the Maker of heaven and earth. He will not let your foot slip— he who watches over you will not slumber. The Lord will keep you from all harm— he will watch over your life. (Psalm 121:1-3,7)

Worship Almighty God who never sleeps, but watches over your life day and night to keep you from all harm.

❷ PRAYER OF *Confession*

For he himself is our peace. He came and preached peace to you who were far away and peace to those who were near. For through him we both have access to the Father by one Spirit. (Ephesians 2:14, 17-18)

Come to the Father through His Son Jesus, the Prince of Peace. Confess your sins and receive God's forgiveness.

❸ PRAYER OF *Petition*

"In this world you will have trouble. But take heart! I have overcome the world." (John 16:33)

And the peace of God, which transcends all understanding, will guard your hearts and your minds in Christ Jesus. (Philippians 4:7)

Peace I leave with you; my peace I give you. I do not give to you as the world gives. Do not let your hearts be troubled and do not be afraid. (John 14:27)

Although the Pilgrims lived in tumultuous times, they never lost hope because they were anchored in God's peace. As believers, we also live in a time of unrest. If you struggle with stress or anxiety, examine your own heart. Ask the Holy Spirit to help you identify the root causes of your concerns, and ask the Lord for healing. Ask God to help you shift your attention away from the things of this world — and develop an abiding trust in Him. Immerse yourself in God's word daily to be transformed and renewed (Romans 12:2).

4 PRAYER OF *Intercession*

Bless those who persecute you; bless and do not curse. Rejoice with those who rejoice; mourn with those who mourn. Live in harmony with one another. Do not be proud, but be willing to associate with people of low position. Do not be conceited. Do not repay anyone evil for evil. Be careful to do what is right in the eyes of everyone. If it is possible, as far as it depends on you, live at peace with everyone. (Romans 12:14-18)

I rejoiced with those who said to me, "Let us go to the house of the Lord." Pray for the peace of Jerusalem: "May those who love you be secure. May there be peace within your walls and security within your citadels." For the sake of the house of the Lord our God, I will seek your prosperity. (Psalm 122:1, 6-7, 9)

From the Mayflower Compact to their peace treaty with Chief Massasoit, the Pilgrims demonstrated a sincere commitment to building unity and fostering peace. Ask God to raise up peacemakers in our nation; leaders who seek peace and pursue it. Pray for the Body of Christ. In a world overrun by fear and division, pray that the global church would demonstrate a peace and unity that commands attention — and points the world to Jesus. Pray for God's peace to manifest in the lives of those He shows you; pray for the peace of Jerusalem.

5 PRAYER OF *Thanksgiving*

But he was pierced for our transgressions, he was crushed for our iniquities; the punishment that brought us peace was on him, and by his wounds we are healed. (Isaiah 53:5)

"Though the mountains be shaken and the hills be removed, yet my unfailing love for you will not be shaken nor my covenant of peace be removed," says the Lord, who has compassion on you. (Isaiah 54:10)

Thank God the Father for his unfailing love and covenant of peace; thank Jesus our Savior, for enduring our punishment on the cross — and bringing us peace.

Turn from evil *and* do good; seek *peace* and pursue it.

(Psalm 34:14)

97

Tyranny

In 17th century England, "the prisons of London were crammed with innocent people whose only crime was the sincerity of their Christian faith. Without benefit of habeas corpus, they had been thrown into jail by any bishop who suspected their nonconformity."[75] As Separatists, the Pilgrims were rooted out by government spies, or worse, they were betrayed by close family members or friends. Once captured, these prisoners were thrown into jail cells "so foul, so disease-ridden, that few could survive an extended stay. With nothing but filthy straw to lie on, with no provision for human waste, no heat, and indifferent or positively rotten food, the strongest man soon succumbed."[76]

The ruling powers stopped at nothing to capture those who dared to defy them. "In order to convict imprisoned Separatist preachers, the bishops were willing to go beyond the bounds of fair play. In London, forty-two preachers were employed as detectives to visit the prisoners, engage them in conversation and try to lure them into saying something that could be used as evidence against them."[77] Even minor offenses could bring severe punishment. One man, George Cotton, was imprisoned for 27 months without trial for the crime of hearing Scripture read in the home of a friend.

Describing the tyranny of their beloved homeland, William Bradford wrote how the Pilgrims were "hunted and persecuted on every side, until their former afflictions were but as fleabitings in comparison. Some were clapped into prison; others had their houses watched night and day, and escaped with difficulty; and most were obliged to fly, and leave their homes and means of livelihood. Yet these and many other even severer trials which afterwards befell them, being only what they expected, they were able to bear by the assistance of God's grace and spirit."[78]

For some, the path of God's grace led to martyrdom. In 1593, the Church of England was eager to silence a young Welsh Separatist preacher named John Penry. After several early brushes with the law, Penry was eventually arrested for preaching in a Separatist church. While he was in jail, church officials ransacked his home for evidence of a capital crime to justify his execution, and they found nothing. But while rifling through his personal papers, they discovered an unpublished draft of a letter Penry was writing to the queen. Seizing their opportunity, the authorities declared Penry's petition to be

ABOUT: To the left of *Liberty's* pedestal, *Tyranny* is revealed as a defeated foe, crushed under the heel of the conquering hero.

offensive to the Crown, and they charged him with sedition. He spent just two months in prison. Ignoring Penry's pleas to be permitted to say good-bye to his wife and four young daughters, his enemies put him to death. He was taken to a public square in London and hanged.

Pastor John Robinson cited Penry as one of many "martyrs of Nonconformity... who had sealed [their] testimony for truth and conscience... [and were] tortured, not accepting deliverance, and stand high on the roll of martyr fame."[79]

Although the Pilgrims desired to live in peace, they were inspired by the accounts in John Foxe's *Actes and Monuments,* later titled *Foxe's Book of Martyrs,* of many faithful believers who glorified the name of Christ with their last breath. Despite their own difficult trials and heartbreaking losses, the Pilgrims remained steadfast in their testimony of God's faithful nature and prevailing goodness.

"What, then, could now sustain them but the spirit of God, and His grace? Ought not the children of their fathers rightly to say: Our fathers were Englishmen who came over the great ocean, and were ready to perish in this wilderness; but they cried unto the Lord, and He heard their voice, and looked on their adversity... Let them therefore praise the Lord, because He is good, and His mercies endure forever. Yea, let them that have been redeemed of the Lord, show how He hath delivered them from the hand of the oppressor... Let them confess before the Lord His loving kindness, and His wonderful works before the sons of men!"[80]

❶ PRAYER OF *Worship*

Lord, you are my God; I will exalt you and praise your name, for in perfect faithfulness you have done wonderful things, things planned long ago. (Isaiah 25:1)

I will praise you, Lord my God, with all my heart; I will glorify your name forever. For great is your love toward me; you have delivered me from the depths, from the realm of the dead. (Psalm 86:12-13)

Magnify the Lord your God, for His perfect faithfulness, who delivers you from death to life.

❷ PRAYER OF *Confession*

Come and hear, all you who fear God; let me tell you what he has done for me. I cried out to him with my mouth; his praise was on my tongue. If I had cherished sin in my heart, the Lord would not have listened; but God has surely listened and has heard my prayer. Praise be to God, who has not rejected my prayer or withheld his love from me! (Psalm 66:16-20)

Ask the Holy Spirit to search your heart for any hidden areas of sin, and seek forgiveness. Be cleansed and refreshed, and praise God for love and mercy.

❸ PRAYER OF *Petition*

Pray for us that the message of the Lord may spread rapidly... that we may be delivered from wicked and evil people, for not everyone has faith. But the Lord is faithful, and he will strengthen you and protect you from the evil one. May the Lord direct your hearts into God's love and Christ's perseverance. (2 Thessalonians 3:1-3,5)

May your whole spirit, soul and body be kept blameless at the coming of our Lord Jesus Christ. The one who calls you is faithful, and he will do it. (1 Thessalonians 5:23-24)

But even if you should suffer for what is right, you are blessed. "Do not fear their threats; do not be frightened." But in your hearts revere Christ as Lord. (1 Peter 3:14-15)

As a prisoner for the Lord, then, I urge you to live a life worthy of the calling you have received. Be completely humble and gentle; be patient, bearing with one another in love. Make every effort to keep the unity of the Spirit through the bond of peace. There is one body and one Spirit, just as you were called to one hope when you were called. (Ephesians 4:1-4)

The Pilgrims held fast to God's word in the face of tyranny and were inspired by brave martyrs who professed Christ to their death. Those who profess a biblical worldview are being challenged in our nation today, and religious persecution is rapidly increasing. Spend some time before the Lord examining your own walk of faith in this hour. Ask God to help you live a life worthy of your calling — even to suffer for what is right — in a culture that is hostile to Christ. When your times of testing come, ask the Holy Spirit to strengthen and protect you from the evil one. Pray for perseverance and a heart that reveres Christ as Lord.

4 PRAYER OF *Intercession*

May God arise, may his enemies be scattered; may his foes flee before him. Praise be to the Lord, to God our Savior, who daily bears our burdens. Our God is a God who saves. (Psalm 68:1,19-20)

Defend the weak and the fatherless; uphold the cause of the poor and the oppressed. Rescue the weak and the needy; deliver them from the hand of the wicked. (Psalm 82:3-4)

When the servant of the man of God got up and went out early the next morning, an army with horses and chariots had surrounded the city. "Oh no, my lord! What shall we do?" the servant asked. "Don't be afraid," the prophet answered. "Those who are with us are more than those who are with them." And Elisha prayed, "Open his eyes, Lord, so that he may see." Then the Lord opened the servant's eyes, and he looked and saw the hills full of horses and chariots of fire all around Elisha. (2 Kings 6:15-17)

For our struggle is not against flesh and blood, but against the rulers, against the authorities, against the powers of this dark world and against the spiritual forces of evil in the heavenly realms. (Ephesians 6:12)

Pray for the people God puts on your heart who are weak and oppressed. Pray for those who are being persecuted for their faith, who are taking a principled stand for Christ in today's godless culture. Ask the Commander of the army of the Lord to release an angelic host to battle on behalf of His children. Pray for God's global Church, including your own church. Ask the Lord to raise up courageous leaders who will proclaim God's Word — and refuse to compromise or be silent. Ask God to open our eyes to what cannot be seen in the natural; to give the Body of Christ divine strategies for spiritual warfare that will yield an eternal harvest.

❺ PRAYER OF *Thanksgiving*

"Hear me, you who know what is right, you people who have taken my instruction to heart: Do not fear the reproach of mere mortals or be terrified by their insults. For the moth will eat them up like a garment; the worm will devour them like wool. But my righteousness will last forever, my salvation through all generations." (Isaiah 51:7-8)

Thank God for His righteousness, which lasts forever.

"May God arise...
Our God is a *God*
who saves.

(Psalm 68:1,20)

FAITH

NATIONAL
❀
MONUMENT
TO THE
FOREFATHERS.
ERECTED
BY A
GRATEFUL PEOPLE
IN REMEMBRANCE OF
THEIR
LABORS, SACRIFICES
AND SUFFERINGS
FOR THE
CAUSE OF CIVIL
AND
RELIGIOUS LIBERTY.

PEACE

PROPHET

By now, I hope you've experienced the same deep appreciation for the Pilgrims that I gained when I first began working on my book, _Forefathers Monument Guidebook._ When I started my research, I had a sense of who the Pilgrims were in history, but little understanding of who they were as a people, something that's often lost in the modern caricature of tall black hats, turkeys, and belt buckles.

I am blessed to live in historic Plymouth, Massachusetts, not far from where the Pilgrims first built their homes and buried their dead. Reading Bradford's journals, Pastor Robinson's letters, and sifting through countless books written generations ago — Plymouth Colony came alive for me. I was captivated by the people I encountered. Strip away the era and circumstances, and the Pilgrims were simply Bible-believing Christians like us who had committed their lives to God and His divine purposes.

In 2020, as I worked to make my publishing deadline, it felt like the America I knew was imploding during the pandemic. Liquor stores, grocery stores, and abortion clinics were all open for business, while churches were forced to close their doors or face heavy fines and government persecution. I was stunned to see video footage of Canadian pastor Artur Pawlowski being handcuffed and dragged away by police. Watching events like this unfold in a modern era personalized the Pilgrim story. I had grown up with the assurance of liberty in this nation. For the first time in my life, I saw Americans being ostracized and persecuted for their faith — a condition that, since then, has dramatically increased.

The 2019 film _A Hidden Life_ tells the story of Franz Jägerstätter, an Austrian farmer and devout Catholic who refused to swear allegiance to Hitler during the rise of the Third Reich. In the movie, Franz agonizes over what his decision will mean for him and his young family. Ultimately, he decides: "If God gives us free will, we're responsible for what we do… or fail to do. I can't do what I believe is wrong. I have to stand up to evil."

As with the Separatist martyr John Penry in 1593, Jägerstätter's principled stand would cost him his life. In 1943, 350 years after Penry was hanged for treason in London, Jägerstätter was executed; he also left behind a wife and three young daughters. Each man, in his own generation and distinct circumstances, wrestled with God in his personal "valley of decision." Each man left a legacy that speaks to this day.

Author Rod Dreher writes: "We will know when we act– or fail to act – as Christians when to be faithful costs us something. It may be a small thing at first– a place on a sports team because we won't play on Sunday mornings, or the respect of our peers when we will not march in a parade for a political cause. But the demands made on us will grow greater, and the consequences for failing to submit to the world's demands will grow more severe... We serve a God who created all things for a purpose. He has shown us in the Bible, especially the Gospels, who we are and how we are to live... He does not want admirers; He wants followers."[81]

The Pilgrims of 1620 are a powerful example for believers in this hour of what it looks like to follow Christ no matter the cost. Bound by covenant, with their faces set as flint, the Pilgrims were determined to obey God over man's laws, opinions, or punishment. Though they were few in number, God used their obedience to fashion new wineskins for an entire nation. "The treasured liberties championed by America's Founding Fathers were in huge measure part of their heritage from the *Mayflower* Pilgrims. Their biblically based values and principles would become the foundation of the United States of America."[82]

In the book of Hebrews, we are encouraged: "Therefore, since we are surrounded by such a great cloud of witnesses, let us throw off everything that hinders and the sin that so easily entangles. And let us run with perseverance the race marked out for us, fixing our eyes on Jesus, the pioneer and perfecter of faith" (Hebrews 12:1-2). The Pilgrim men and women of Scrooby, Leiden, and Plymouth Colony now join the great cloud of witnesses who have gone before us in the faith. God set them in their hour of His church on earth – and they ran their race well.

In creating this devotional, I hope their story has inspired you. But even more than that, I hope you see *yourself* in God's story. Our Lord Jesus said: "Whoever believes in me will do the works I have been doing, and they will do even greater things than these" (John 14:12). We are not here by accident. God has placed us in this present generation to do even greater works for His glory. He has given each of us gifts, talents, and a measure of faith to accomplish His divine purpose for our lives. What will *your* legacy be?

As you consider your answer, know that God can do more through a humble heart and surrendered life than we could ever ask or imagine (see Ephesians 3:20).

The great irony of the Forefathers Monument is that if the Pilgrims could see it today, they would shrink back in humility before this soaring, 81-foot-tall tribute. Yet, these earthly accomplishments are the very crowns they will one day cast at our Lord's feet. As brothers and sisters in the Lord, let us spur one another on to love and good deeds. With our eyes fixed firmly on Christ, let us glorify God with the sum of our lives. May we all run our race well, and gather many crowns to cast at His feet.

"To him who is able to keep you from stumbling and to present you before his glorious presence without fault and with great joy – to the only God our Savior be glory, majesty, power and authority, through Jesus Christ our Lord, before all ages, now and forevermore! Amen" (Jude 1:24-25).

BELOW: The view from Burial Hill in Plymouth, Massachusetts, where many of the early Pilgrims are buried, including Governor William Bradford, and William and Mary Brewster.

① PRAYER OF *Worship*

The Lord is exalted, for he dwells on high; he will fill Zion with his justice and righteousness. He will be the sure foundation for your times, a rich store of salvation and wisdom and knowledge; the fear of the Lord is the key to this treasure. (Isaiah 33:5-6)

"Yours, Lord, is the greatness and the power and the glory and the majesty and the splendor, for everything in heaven and earth is yours. Yours, Lord, is the kingdom; you are exalted as head over all." (1 Chronicles 29:11)

Worship the Lord, full of power and glory, and the sure foundation of our times.

② PRAYER OF *Confession*

My dear children, I write this to you so that you will not sin. But if anybody does sin, we have an advocate with the Father—Jesus Christ, the Righteous One. He is the atoning sacrifice for our sins, and not only for ours but also for the sins of the whole world. We know that we have come to know him if we keep his commands. Whoever says, "I know him," but does not do what he commands is a liar, and the truth is not in that person. But if anyone obeys his word, love for God is truly made complete in them. This is how we know we are in him: Whoever claims to live in him must live as Jesus did. (1 John 2:1-6)

Confess your sins with a contrite heart, and receive forgiveness. Rededicate yourself to following Christ in word and deed, and to live as Jesus did.

③ PRAYER OF *Petition*

"Do not suppose that I have come to bring peace to the earth. I did not come to bring peace, but a sword. For I have come to turn 'a man against his father, a daughter against her mother, a daughter-in-law against her mother-in-law – a man's enemies will be the members of his own household.' Anyone who loves their father or mother more than me is not worthy of me; anyone who loves their son or daughter more than me is not worthy of me. Whoever does not take up their cross and follow me is not worthy of me. Whoever finds their life will lose it, and whoever loses their life for my sake will find it." (Matthew 10:34–37)

Now when David had served God's purpose in his own generation, he fell asleep; he was buried with his ancestors. (Acts 13:36)

Ask God to speak to you concerning your spiritual legacy. Seek the Lord over what He has created you to do in this life; consider the best use of your gifts and talents to further God's kingdom. If you've been resisting the Lord in a certain area due to fear or insecurity, repent; ask the Holy Spirit for the courage to step out in obedience. If you're unsure of how God wants to use you, ask the Lord to show you; get wise counsel from a pastor or a mature Christian friend who can pray with you. If you've been held back by the opinions of family members or friends — admit your fears to the Lord. Humble yourself. Pray for the strength to serve God's purpose in your lifetime, and to follow Christ no matter the cost.

④ PRAYER OF *Intercession*

The apostles were brought in and made to appear before the Sanhedrin to be questioned by the high priest. "We gave you strict orders not to teach in this name," he said. "Yet you have filled Jerusalem with your teaching and are determined to make us guilty of this man's blood." Peter and the other apostles replied: "We must obey God rather than human beings!" (Acts 5:27-29)

We live in an hour when people of faith are being criticized and attacked for having a biblical worldview in our nation. Pray for the Lord's Church in America and around the globe. Ask the Holy Spirit to fill God's people with a Christian zeal that reflects Christ in word and deed and obeys God over man.

⑤ PRAYER OF *Thanksgiving*

Who shall separate us from the love of Christ? Shall trouble or hardship or persecution or famine or nakedness or danger or sword? As it is written: "For your sake we face death all day long; we are considered as sheep to be slaughtered." No, in all these things we are more than conquerors through him who loved us. For I am convinced that neither death nor life, neither angels nor demons, neither the present nor the future, nor any powers, neither height nor depth, nor anything else in all creation, will be able to separate us from the love of God that is in Christ Jesus our Lord. (Romans 8:35-39)

Thank God that nothing can separate us from the love of Christ Jesus our Lord.

ENDNOTES:

1. Bradford, William. *The History Of Plymouth Colony. Pub. For The Classics Club By W.J. Black,* 1948, p.10.
2. *Ibid., p.6.*
3. *Ibid., p.30.*
4. Bradford, William. *Bradford's History Of The Plymouth Settlement, 1608-1650. E.P. Dutton & Co.,* 1920, p. 65.
5. *Ibid., p. 83.*
6. Sheets, Dutch. *Give Him 15. Vol. 1, Dutch Sheets Ministries,* 25 Nov. 2022, pp. 114–115.
7. *"Founders Online: From John Adams To Massachusetts Militia, 11 October 1798". Founders.Archives.Gov,* 2020.
8. Robinson, John. *The Works Of John Robinson, Pastor Of The Pilgrim Fathers, Vol. I. Reed And Pardon,* 1851, p. 34.
9. Paget, Harold. *Bradford's History Of The Plymouth Settlement. E.P. Dutton & Company,* 1920, p.15.
10. *Ibid., p.17.*
11. Bradford, William. *Bradford's History Of The Plymouth Settlement, 1608-1650. E.P. Dutton & Co.,* 1920, p. 203.
12. Bartlett, Robert Merrill. *The Faith Of The Pilgrims. United Church Press,* 1978, p.171.
13. Paget, Harold. *Bradford's History Of The Plymouth Settlement. E.P. Dutton & Company,* 1920, p. 21.
14. Medved, Michael. *The American Miracle. 1st ed., Crown Forum,* 2016, p. 46.
15. Robinson, John. *The Works of John Robinson, Pastor of the Pilgrim Fathers. Vol. 1, London, J. Snow,* 1851, p. 45
16. Bartlett, Robert Merrill. *The Faith Of The Pilgrims. United Church Press,* 1978, p.50
17. Bradford, William. *Bradford's History Of The Plymouth Settlement, 1608-1650. E.P. Dutton & Co.,* 1920, p. 7.
18. *Ibid., p. 110*
19. Bradford, William. *The History Of Plymouth Colony. W.J. Black,* 1948, p.10
20. *Ibid., p.13*
21. Federer, William J. *The Original 13. Amerisearch Incorporated,* 1 Oct. 2006, p. 95.
22. Bradford, William. *Bradford's History Of The Plymouth Settlement, 1608-1650. E.P. Dutton & Co.,* 1920, p. 7.
23. *Ibid., p. 28.*
24. *Ibid., p. 76.*
25. *Ibid., p. 55-56.*
26. *Ibid, p. 76.*
27. Willison, George F. *Saints & Strangers. Parnassus Imprints,* 1945, p. 166.
28. Bradford, William. *The History Of Plymouth Colony. W.J. Black,* 1948, p. 102.
29. *Ibid., p.104.*
30. Bradford, William. *Bradford's History Of The Plymouth Settlement, 1608-1650. E.P. Dutton & Co.,* 1920, p. xx.
31. *Ibid., p. 293.*
32. Bradford, William. *The History Of Plymouth Colony. W.J. Black,* 1948, p. 363
33. Bradford, William. *Bradford's History Of The Plymouth Settlement, 1608-1650. E.P. Dutton & Co.,* 1920, p. 294.
34. Bradford, William. *The History Of Plymouth Colony. W.J. Black,* 1948, p.364
35. Federer, William J. *America's God and Country : Encyclopedia of Quotations. St. Louis, Mo, Amerisearch Inc,* 2000, p. 83.
36. Bartlett, Robert Merrill. *The Faith Of The Pilgrims. United Church Press,* 1978, p.45.
37. *Ibid., p.43.*
38. *"Education In Colonial America | Robert A. Peterson". Fee.Org,* 2020, https://fee.org/article/education-in-colonial-america/.
39. Cremin, Lawrence A. *American Education: The Colonial Experience, 1607-1783. Harper Torchbooks,* 1970, p. 40.
40. *"Education In Colonial America | Robert A. Peterson". Fee.Org,* 2020, https://fee.org/articles/education-in-colonial-america/.
41. Cremin, Lawrence A. *American Education: The Colonial Experience, 1607-1783. Harper Torchbooks,* 1970, p.51.
42. *"Education In Colonial America | Robert A. Peterson". Fee.Org,* 2020, https://fee.org/articles/education-in-colonial-america/.
43. Newcombe, Jerry. *The Book That Made America. Nordskog Pub., Inc.,* 2009, p. 105.
44. Robinson, John. *The Works of John Robinson, Pastor of the Pilgrim Fathers. Vol. 3, London, J. Snow,* 1851, p. 103.
45. Bradford, William. *Bradford's History Of The Plymouth Settlement, 1608-1650. E.P. Dutton & Co.,* 1920, p. 55.
46. Bradford, William. *The History Of Plymouth Colony. W.J. Black,* 1948, p.72.
47. Bartlett, Robert Merrill. *The Faith Of The Pilgrims. United Church Press,* 1978, pp. 155-156.
48. *Ibid., p. 156.*
49. Smith, Bradford. *Bradford Of Plymouth. 1st ed., Lippincott,* 1951, p. 320.
50. *Ibid., p. 319.*
51. Bradford, William. *The History Of Plymouth Colony. W.J. Black,* 1948, p. 110.

52. Smith, Bradford. *Bradford Of Plymouth.* 1st ed., Lippincott, 1951, p. 320.
53. Gragg, Rod. *The Pilgrim Chronicles.* Regnery Publishing, 2014, p. 93.
54. Bradford, William. *Bradford's History Of The Plymouth Settlement, 1608-1650.* E.P. Dutton & Co., 1920, p. 20-21.
55. *Ibid., p. 21.*
56. Bartlett, Robert Merrill. *The Faith Of The Pilgrims.* United Church Press, 1978, p. 99.
57. *Ibid., p.89.*
58. *Ibid.*
59. *Ibid.*
60. Gragg, Rod. *The Pilgrim Chronicles.* Regnery Publishing, 2014, p. 288.
61. Bartlett, Robert Merrill. *The Faith Of The Pilgrims.* United Church Press, 1978, p.149.
62. Bradford, William. *Bradford's History Of The Plymouth Settlement, 1608-1650.* E.P. Dutton & Co., 1920, p. 116.
63. *Ibid., p. 116.*
64. *Ibid., p. 115.*
65. Smith, Bradford. *Bradford Of Plymouth.* 1st ed., Lippincott, 1951, p. 20-21.
66. Gragg, Rod. *The Pilgrim Chronicles.* Regnery Publishing, 2014, p. 291.
67. *https://www.archives.gov/founding-docs/declaration-transcript*
68. Kistler, Charles E. *This Nation under God.* Boston, Richard G. Badger, Publisher, The Gorham Press, 1924, p. 71
69. *Ibid.*
70. Young, Alexander. *Chronicles Of The Pilgrim Fathers Of The Colony Of Plymouth, From 1602 To 1625.* 2nd ed., C.C. Little And J. Brown, 1844, p. 355.
71. Bradford, William. *Bradford's History Of The Plymouth Settlement, 1608-1650.* E.P. Dutton & Co., 1920, p. 314.
72. *Ibid., p. 315.*
73. *Ibid., p.54.*
74. Goodwin, Henry Martyn. *The Pilgrim Fathers: A Glance at Their History, Character and Principles, in Two Memorial Discourses, Delivered in the First Congregational Church, May 22, 1870.*
75. Smith, Bradford. *Bradford Of Plymouth.* 1st ed., Lippincott, 1951, p. 61-62.
76. *Ibid., p. 32.*
77. *Ibid., p.62.*
78. Bradford, William. *Bradford's History Of The Plymouth Settlement, 1608-1650.* E.P. Dutton & Co., 1920, p. 8.
79. Robinson, John. *The Works of John Robinson, Pastor of the Pilgrim Fathers.* Vol. 3, London, J. Snow, 1851, p. 356.
80. Bradford, William. *Bradford's History Of The Plymouth Settlement, 1608-1650.* E.P. Dutton & Co., 1920, p. 66.
81. Dreher, Rod. *Live Not By Lies: A Manual for Christian Dissidents,* Penguin Books, 2022, p. 163.
82. Gragg, Rod. *The Pilgrim Chronicles.* Regnery Publishing, 2014, p. 291

PHOTO CREDITS:

14, 15 — Courtesy of Dustin Fleming

31, 63, 71 — Courtesy of Debra Riservato

Front and back cover, 6, 12, 13, 16, 19, 23, 26, 29, 33, 36, 38, 41, 44, 46, 51, 52, 55, 59, 62, 64, 67, 70, 72, 78, 81, 87, 88, 90, 96, 98, 104, 107, 111, 114, 116, 122, 124, 127, 130, 138 — Courtesy of Sojourner Media, visit: www.sojourner-media.com

GOD'S PLAN FOR SALVATION

"There is no one righteous, not even one." (Romans 3:10)

For the wages of sin is death, but the gift of God is eternal life in Christ Jesus our Lord. (Romans 6:23)

For God so loved the world that he gave his one and only Son, that whoever believes in him shall not perish but have eternal life. (John 3:16)

If you declare with your mouth, "Jesus is Lord," and believe in your heart that God raised him from the dead, you will be saved. (Romans 10:9)

HOW CAN I RECEIVE ETERNAL LIFE?

Our sin separates us from a holy, righteous God. But God sent His Son, Jesus, to pay the price for our sins— so that we could be forgiven and have our relationship with Him restored. We can't earn salvation; it's a free gift of God's grace that we receive by placing our faith in Jesus Christ. To receive salvation, admit that you are a sinner; repent, and turn away from your sins. Confess that Jesus Christ died on the cross for your sins and was raised from the dead; ask Him to be Lord of your life. As a follower of Christ, do your best to live according to God's Word. Below is a simple prayer you can pray to invite Jesus into your heart:

Prayer of Faith

"God, I admit that I am a sinner. I believe Your Son Jesus died for my sins, and that He was raised from the dead. Forgive me for my sins. From this day forward, I have decided to place my faith in Jesus—and follow Him as my Lord and Savior. God, fill me with Your Holy Spirit and teach me how to live for You. I pray this in the name of Jesus. Amen."

Intercessors for America

You may be stirred to action after reading this book, just as IFA's founders were stirred by the revolutionary teachings of Derek Prince on the shaping of our nation through prayer and fasting. In 1973, this group of six believers heeded the call and took a step of faith to invite others to participate. IFA was chartered in the nation's cradle, in Plymouth, Massachusetts. One of the first official activities of the organization took place at the large dining table in the Plymouth home of John and Rosalin Talcott, where they wrote, assembled, and mailed a prayer letter to a group of like-minded people who recognized the need for God to intervene in U.S. governmental and cultural issues. From these beginnings, IFA has grown into a nationwide network of hundreds of thousands of Christians who are praying for our nation.

NEWS. PRAYER. ACTION.

NEWS *that the legacy media isn't talking about, to help you pray more strategically*

Hundreds of **PRAYER** *opportunities, for elected officials, national and state issues, and even for fellow intercessors*

Take **ACTION** *on critical issues and send messages easily to elected officials*

Find more at
IFApray.org

Intercessors for America (IFA) is a 501(c)(3) ministry organization.

Monumental
PRAYERS

WAS INSPIRED AND ADAPTED FROM MATERIAL FEATURED IN THE
FOREFATHERS MONUMENT GUIDEBOOK

We hope you have enjoyed this inspiring devotional on the legacy of the Pilgrims revealed through the Forefathers Monument. To discover more about the history and symbolism of this national landmark, and learn how the Pilgrim's Christian faith influenced America's roots, order your copy of the *Forefathers Monument Guidebook* today!

Praise for the
FOREFATHERS MONUMENT GUIDEBOOK

I cannot recommend *Forefathers Monument Guidebook* enough. In this day when revisionist history dominates education and tourism, we need reliable sources of information about our historical treasures. That's what this is. Even if you can't visit Plymouth, Massachusetts, you can enjoy this incredible monument and what it represents through this beautiful book. - **DAVE KUBAL**, *President/CEO, Intercessors for America*

I have studied and led tours of this statue for 40 years, and what Michelle Gallagher has done in her *Forefathers Monument Guidebook* is phenomenal. Her weaving of the history of the monument as it is intertwined with the history of the Pilgrims brings the monument to life. This is more than a table book; it is a pictorial guide into America's Hometown roots and our national fabric. America was founded on unique ideas which, when pondered and practiced over consecutive generations, produce the kind of liberty that protects religious and civil expression. What is best, these ideas, drawn from the Bible, advance by voluntary consent and not by conquest. I highly recommend every American carefully read this book and do so with the intention of influencing their neighbors, fellow co-workers, children, and grandchildren! - **DR. PAUL JEHLE**, *President, Plymouth Rock Foundation*

Pastors, politicians, presidents, principals, and parents have all benefitted from this beautifully illustrated and thoroughly researched guidebook. I have referred to its pages over and over to deepen my personal understanding and more accurately teach the monumental message of our own American 'Gilgal' stone, pointing us as citizens back to the sacred beginnings of our biblically based republic and the timeless principles that will be her revival. - **KIRK CAMERON**, *actor, author, and filmmaker*